Pot Holes, Stinky Stuff, and Thin Blankets

Pot Holes, Stinky Stuff, and Thin Blankets

THE ~~MILES~~ smiles THAT TAKE US HOME

PAULA HILL

AND DAUGHTERS MELINDA HILL MANESS AND TARA HILL SHARPE

ISBN: 978-1-64288-026-7

Copyright © 2018 by Tim Hill Ministries,
Cleveland, Tennessee 37320

Printed in the United States of America

Dedication

A special blessing is contained inside this book in the form of six very wonderfully inspired devotional offerings written by my oldest and youngest daughters. Both are well qualified and able to write their own books if given the time and opportunity. I see in them the heart of the Father and I think you may, as well. Thanks, Girls! I am very proud of what you have written and the experiences your words represent.

I would also like to dedicate this book to all those out there who have spoken to me of the encouragement that has come from my previous books, *Heart Songs* and *Grace Notes*. Your words have inspired me to want to continue with another book. To everyone who has unknowingly given me the material for this project by way of speaking a kind word or telling me a story that caused me to think about something I otherwise wouldn't have considered, I thank you too. I love talking to other people about their families and their life's journeys. It reminds me that everyone is human and we all walk this road together.

I especially want to thank my husband for his encouragement. A special appreciation to you, Tim. You never criticize, but just simply try to help me communicate in a better way. I'm very grateful for that. It was through your encouragement the first book ever came to be. Now, here I am with the third book and this time two of our daughters have contributed to the writing, as well.

To my daughter Brittany, while you may have not written a story with pen in hand, you are very much a part of every story because you are part of me. You are woven into the fabric of our family. Certainly by birth, but even more by love, faith, and hope. The miles of life became the smiles of life on many occasions because of you.

Finally, to the reader—pastors' wives, leaders' companions, and that marvelous sisterhood of prayer warriors—I write because of you. You inspire me to keep reaching and loving. As long as you are there, I'll be here, looking for every lesson at every turn.

—Paula Hill

Contents

Foreword

Paula Hill has dedicated her life to inspiring and helping others as a committed intercessor, a trusted counselor, a dedicated minister's wife, mother to three daughters and Nana to five wonderful grandchildren. In recent years, she has touched the world as a sought-after conference speaker and author. Traveling extensively around the world, she has made a global impact from Asia to Africa and Europe to South America, having touched down in more than 100 nations of the world, praying, speaking, and just loving people.

Those travels have brought her innumerable experiences that have become the inspirational stories and lessons now told in three different devotional volumes. Stories from more than 40 years of traveling the roads with her husband as evangelists and church leaders. Stories of roads filled with pot holes that led to lumpy hotel beds barely covered by what seemed to be paper-thin blankets. Stories that remind us that even when life just stinks, you just laugh at the laughable, learn from the learnable, and keep on loving until that same road leads you home.

Paula's stories are as real as she is, as are stories written and told by her daughters, Melinda and Tara. The lessons from these two "next generation" moms are just as genuine and filled with wisdom and insight.

These three women of God invite readers into the living room of their hearts to see their families up close and personal and learn from their laughter and tears, mistakes and triumphs, and especially the miles and smiles of the long, long journey leading them home.

—Joni Lamb
Daystar Television Network

Acknowledgments

I would like to thank several wonderful people who have worked so hard in helping with this book.

Dee Raff—for the many months serving as managing editor while never neglecting other duties and responsibilities. Thank you, Dee. Amazing friend.

Janet Price—for serving as proofing editor and making sure things were as they should be. You're great.

Adam Aziz—for graphic and layout design. You have given my book the look that helps tell the stories even before they're read on the page.

Tom George—for doing the final edit, designing the inside pages, and coordinating the production of the book. Tim and I haven't done one without you yet.

Tim, Melinda, Brittany, and Tara—the family who loves, laughs, sings, and writes. As someone once said, "It takes a village," and my little village always comes through.

Of course, it couldn't happen without my adorable grandchildren who give me so much material. I love you Brayden, Hailey, Lucas, and Jaxon—and one on the way.

My deepest appreciation to all.

Introduction

I t's hard to believe contained between these covers is a third devotional book. I never knew or believed there would ever be even one, much less three.

If you've followed the writings in *Heart Songs* and *Grace Notes*, you've picked up on the fact that I journal about everyday life lessons. I realized long ago that it is the way in which God speaks to me and teaches me what I need to remember or brings to me a new lesson I need to learn. Because of this, there will always be much more material contained in my mind and in my spirit than will ever be inside the pages of a book.

I will never stop observing and listening for the prompts from the Holy Spirit to lead me and guide me through life. Several devotions are contained here from Melinda and Tara, my oldest and youngest daughters. They are on their own personal journeys, too, and hopefully I have had some influence upon them to learn their lessons as well through the triumphs and failings of motherhood, being a godly wife, friendships, and living every day with an openness to watch and learn.

My prayer is once again that you will see yourself in these devotions and situations, and I ask the heavenly Father to use them to bless you and speak directly to your heart. I believe most, if not all of you, could share powerful truths of your spiritual journey as well and even more succinctly than I have done. Sometimes, you don't need to hear anything deep or theological—just real life, and that is what I've attempted to do with this book. Whether you read one devotion a week or the whole book at once does not matter. Just open your heart and pray to see my heart for the Father through the words written on these pages.

—Paula Hill

Potholes

The Lord will keep you from all harm—he will watch over your life (Psalms 121:7 NIV).

I READ ABOUT A MAN IN BRUSSELS, BELGIUM who had started planting flowers in the many potholes in the streets throughout the city. Apparently, the problem was so frustrating he decided to take matters in his own hands in his own humorous way. I found that story comical as I tried to imagine what he would have done if he had been with us on a recent trip.

We were on a short trip from home to where my husband was ministering in an evening service. I was driving so he could make calls and take care of church business without being a distracted driver. Although we were driving on the interstate, there were a few stretches of roadway that were pretty rough, and traffic was heavy. Suddenly, and without warning I hit a HUGE pothole. It was so deep I think it swallowed the three cars behind me. Well, maybe not quite that deep, but you get the picture. It was the Grand Canyon of potholes. It jarred us to the point I hoped my tires hadn't been knocked out of balance. I was watching for the tire light to come on but, thankfully, it never did. The vehicle in front of me, who must have hit the same pothole, didn't even bounce. It seemed to just keep gliding along, but I know they had to feel it inside their car just as we did.

I thought about my spiritual life and experience. Sometimes, it seems like I hit a big pothole in life and I feel

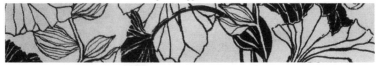

as if I will surely suffer so much damage that I may just not survive without severe impairment. It doesn't matter whether it's emotional, spiritual, or physical damage; some things seem inevitably bound to happen. Here's the hardest part—when I look at others sometimes, whom I know hit the same potholes, they seem to just glide over them like they didn't even happen. I must always remember that what seems to be so on the outside looking in is seldom what it appears to be. I know they feel the jolts just as I do. I also remind myself the vehicle behind me probably didn't see my car shake and tremble either. Why? For one thing, there are these mechanisms called shock absorbers that take the impact of the jolts and jerks a vehicle sustains. So, I have to have good shock absorbers in place in my spiritual life, as well. And I do! There are three of them to be exact: namely the Father, the Son, and the Holy Spirit. They can absorb the impact and I know I will suffer no damage. Praise God!

God, I thank You that You take the sudden impacts in my life and You protect me from harm.

~Paula

My Bible Reading Plan

☐   Day 1   Genesis 1–3
☐   Day 2   Genesis 4–6
☐   Day 3   Genesis 7–9
☐   Day 4   Genesis 10–12
☐   Day 5   Genesis 13–15
☐   Day 6   Genesis 16–18
☐   Day 7   Genesis 19–21

My Prayer Journal

Stinky Stuff

He has made everything beautiful in its time
(Ecclesiastes 3:11 NIV).

I'VE BEEN TOLD THE SENSE OF SMELL is the first of the senses babies use after they are born. It's also been said the average person can detect 10,000 different smells. Powerful memories can be triggered by a scent. The smell of bread or cookies hot from the oven, or bacon and eggs cooking in the morning, or even the smell of burning leaves bring back memories of my childhood to this day. But not all smells are pleasant. In fact, some are just plain nasty!

One day, I came home fo find yard workers outside our home. The smell just about knocked me down. You know the smell of fresh fertilizer if you've been around it. It seems to hang in the air making your eyes water and your nose look for a hiding place. But in the spring and summer, I have beautiful roses, tulips, hostas, and other blooming plants. It is pure joy for me to sit in my sunroom and look outside at the beauty when all these things are in bloom. That's where the fertilizer comes in. The flowers would not be nearly as beautiful if the fertilizer was not spread to give them vitamins and extra nourishment to create beautiful blooms. Oh, I know they would bloom anyway, because that's the natural order of plants, but they would not be as brilliant and healthy without the extra "stuff" the fertilizer gives them.

As I went inside, the thought occurred to me how many times things in our lives literally stink. There are times when we cannot foresee anything fragrant or beautiful coming out

of the smelly situation we find ourselves in, but I am reminded God makes all things beautiful in His time. When those situations are over, we will probably never forget how dirty or unappealing they were, but hopefully we can look back and realize God can and does bring beauty from the not-so-fragrant times in our lives.

Father, I thank You that You will bring a beautiful outcome if we will be patient and let You do Your work in and around us.

~Paula

My Bible Reading Plan

☐ Day 8   Genesis 22–24
☐ Day 9   Genesis 25–27
☐ Day 10   Genesis 28–30
☐ Day 11   Genesis 31–33
☐ Day 12   Genesis 34–36
☐ Day 13   Genesis 37–39
☐ Day 14   Genesis 40–42

My Prayer Journal

Thin Blankets

The bed is too short to stretch out on, the blanket too narrow to wrap around you (Isaiah 28:20 NIV).

ONCE AGAIN, I HAVE EXITED A HOTEL ROOM where I had a hard time resting. Why? Well, here's the thing. On my bed at home I have sheets, a blanket, and a fluffy comforter. I like my bedroom to be cold, and I love to snuggle up with the covers pulled up to my eyeballs. Sweet rest! But many times, in all our travels through the years, with countless nights in hotel rooms, my sleep is disrupted. It's those thin blankets! Not that you could really even call them blankets. They are more like thick sheets. At times I have placed a pile of clothes on top of those so-called blankets for the weight and warmth it brought to me. I've even decided to sleep in my fluffy, thick robe a few times. You can just imagine that, can't you? Did I mention these thin blankets are also too short to pull up around my eyes? I keep scooting down in bed until my feet are dangling close to the edge. So, there I am, thermostat set to "Snow Flurries," wrapped in my fluffy robe, clothes from my suitcase piled on top of me, with my feet hanging off the end of the bed just so I can bring the covers up to my eyelashes! I eventually find my comfort spot—it just takes some extra tossing and turning to get there. It sure makes me appreciate my own bed, though.

Do you ever have trouble resting in God because you feel like He doesn't have you covered quite good enough? Maybe your circumstances right now have left you feeling vulnerable to the cold winds of disappointment or

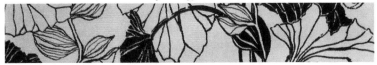

the stark reality of grief. Sometimes, there seems to be nothing or no one that can give us that warm, cozy feeling within our own spiritual lives. The truth is, we feel exposed to the elements spiritually. I have good news. The Father will cover you with all that you need. He will pile on extra layers of blessings and strength just when you think there's no hope in sight. He knows how far we can go and He won't let us go past the point of His provision. God is there all along, we just don't like to be uncomfortable, so we struggle in that place. But, there is rest and peace under the blanket of His love and guidance. He will cover you.

God, I thank You because I'm covered continually under Your grace and mercy. Your love is a constant provision for me. You will not let me be alone.

~Paula

My Bible Reading Plan

☐ Day 15   Genesis 43–45
☐ Day 16   Genesis 46–48
☐ Day 17   Genesis 49–50
☐ Day 18   Exodus 1–3
☐ Day 19   Exodus 4–6
☐ Day 20   Exodus 7–9
☐ Day 21   Exodus 10–12

My Prayer Journal

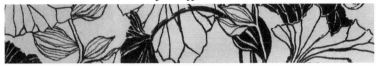

Blessings

The blessing of the Lord, it maketh rich, and he addeth no sorrow with it (Proverbs 10:22 KJV).

ONE THING IN MY LIFE NEVER SEEMS TO GET ANY EASI-
ER. It is when I have the grand privilege to be with parents
or children and grandchildren. No matter how long the
span of time I spend with them, it seems like the moment
I arrive, I start thinking about having to say goodbye soon.
When our girls were younger, they always knew there would
be the possibility somewhere in the future of separation.
As a family, we were always aware that when they reached
adulthood, and knowing we were in ministry, God's will and
plan could take us just about anywhere. What each of us as-
sumed was that we, the parents, would leave them. But the
reason turned out differently than we all imagined, because
our oldest and youngest daughters married ministers, and
our middle daughter graduated from university and moved
away for a job opportunity. I laugh sometimes and ask them:
"Who left whom?"

When I'm in those situations, and my heart and my emotions want to dictate the behavior that says, "just go find a
private place to cry and feel sorry about the situation," I try to
remind myself of all the wonderful blessings that have been
bestowed upon me. Blessings are appreciated more if you
think you weren't going to have them to begin with. Most of
my trips are last minute, when I just seize the opportunity to
jump on an airplane and go for two or three days. I am keen-
ly aware there are many and various situations and circumstances in life that evoke the same kinds of feelings—many
of them much weightier than not having all the time you

long for to visit with children and grandchildren. The aches and longings of the heart can be over family loss, the shattering of plans and dreams, betrayal by someone dear to us, perhaps coming to the sunset years of life and feeling like a big percentage of life was only filled with dissatisfaction and disappointment. There are so many reasons. Life doesn't always feel like the blessing side of the scale is the heaviest side. However, when I survey my situation and really look through eyes that aren't clouded by self-pity or woe is me, I'm always overwhelmed by the goodness and mercy of my heavenly Father. Sometimes, it takes looking through the eyes of faith—eyes that can peer far ahead into the realm of eternal blessings—to be reminded that someday all the things that make the heart heavy will melt into blissful joy and peace when we are at home with our Creator, the beginning and the ending of all blessings and all things good and true.

God, I thank You that you are the author of blessings.
Help me not to be selfish with what You bestow on me.
I will remember to be grateful for all I receive.

~Paula

My Bible Reading Plan

☐	Day 22	Exodus 13–15
☐	Day 23	Exodus 16–18
☐	Day 24	Exodus 19–21
☐	Day 25	Exodus 22–24
☐	Day 26	Exodus 25–27
☐	Day 27	Exodus 28–30
☐	Day 28	Exodus 31–33

My Prayer Journal

Clean

But we are all like an unclean thing, and all our righteousnesses are like filthy rags; We all fade as a leaf, and our iniquities, like the wind, have taken us away (Isaiah 64:6 NKJV).

A popular song we often sing at our church says:

There's nothing too dirty, that you can't make worthy. You washed me in mercy, I am clean.

Later in the song, it says:

Washed in the blood of your sacrifice, Your blood flowed red and made me white. MY DIRTY RAGS ARE PURIFIED. I AM CLEAN!

I've always taken that to mean He cleans up our mistakes, makes us new from our past, and forgives our sins. But recently, as I was singing that song, the Lord placed something in my heart. I started thinking about my kitchen rags. I don't use my kitchen rags to wash the car, or clean mud off my shoes, or wash windows on the outside of the house. They are used for kitchen things: drying dishes, cleaning spills, occasionally protecting my hand from a hot plate. The kitchen rags just become dirty from everyday use and must be washed and made clean.

Imagine you have a spotless past (I know none of us do, but bear with me.) You have no sin, no dirt, no scars. This song may not connect with you, because if you are already clean, why would Jesus need to clean you again? Well, just like those kitchen rags, we are made dirty every day from common use. A little "dirt" here when we take on the hurts of our children, a little bit there when

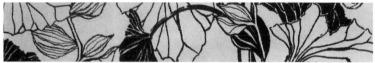

we become worn out from never-ending housework, a little more when we watch the evening news. We become "dirty" from daily use just like those rags. Not dirty in a sinful way, but in a well-used kitchen rag kind of way. Jesus didn't come to only save the horrible sinner, but he came to renew us and daily wash us clean.

The Bible says: "Therefore we do not lose heart. Though outwardly we are wasting away, yet inwardly we are being renewed day by day" (2 Corinthians 4:16 NIV).

Those words hit so much closer to me now, because not only did Jesus cleanse me from my past (because, once again, none of us are spotless), but He cleans me every single day from the dirt of daily use. Aren't you glad that no matter the depth of your "dirty rags," you can be purified and clean again?

Lord, thank you for the gift of salvation that washed me white as snow through the blood of your sacrifice, and thank you for the daily renewal as you refresh me and cleanse me from the daily dirt that comes with life.

~Melinda

My Bible Reading Plan

☐	Day 29	Exodus 34–36
☐	Day 30	Exodus 37–40
☐	Day 31	Leviticus 1–3
☐	Day 32	Leviticus 4–6
☐	Day 33	Leviticus 7–9
☐	Day 34	Leviticus 10–12
☐	Day 35	Leviticus 13–15

My Prayer Journal

Clean Water

*You, God, are my God, earnestly I seek you; I thirst for you,
my whole being longs for you, in a dry and parched land
where there is no water* (Psalms 63:1 NIV).

SEVERAL YEARS AGO, MY HUSBAND AND I were privileged
to serve the Church of God in the ministry of World Missions.
It was an eye-opening experience, to say the least. We will
forever thank God for the opportunity we were given to serve
in such a life-changing role. I quickly realized that what I had
always perceived as the greatest needs on the mission field
were just my perception, and many times it was the wrong
perception. I believed the greatest need was food, clothing,
housing, etc. However, it became evident that clean water
was the greatest need in most of the places we traveled. If
the drinking water is not clean and pure, it brings sickness
and disease that eventually results in slow, painful deaths
as the body shuts down. This is from the effects of basically
consuming poisoned and bitter liquid into the body's sys-
tems. They can no longer function in a healthy manner. So, if
we only provide shelter, clothing, and food alone, as important as those are, we cannot save people. The human body
can survive longer without food than it can without water.
At least 60 percent of the human body is made up of water
and every living cell in the body needs it to keep functioning.
A person can go three weeks without food, but typically the
survival rate is only three to four days without water. Perhaps a maximum of one week, but not in difficult conditions
like broiling heat. Without the provision of water, there is not
much hope for an individual.

I heard a statement that really hit home with me not long ago. It was, "People draw from the well full of bitter waters." How powerful and true that statement is. When, as a child of God, we only dwell on the bad and negative circumstances and situations in life, we become so angry and frustrated that it's absolutely like drawing poison, bitter water up from a well that reeks of disease and death. No nourishment, no hydration, no refreshing, only eventually a spiritual death. How sad and completely unnecessary, because Jesus is the living water full of life and health and strength to our bodies. That's why He speaks to us in His Word about thinking on good things, true things, those that are of a good report. These provide spiritual hydration, and a healthy benefit to our souls. Oh, that we could learn this truth. Our well-being depends on drinking from our Father's well of water which is spiritually refreshing, life giving, replenishing, full of everything we need to not only survive, but thrive.

Oh God, I thirst for You, the living water. Thank You for Your presence in and around me. You give me life.

~Paula

My Bible Reading Plan

My Prayer Journal

Come Find Me

Therefore they inquired of the further, if the man should yet come thither. And the LORD answered, Behold, he has hid himself among the stuff. And they ran and fetched him thence (1 Samuel 10:22-23 KJV).

I AM AMAZED BY THIS PASSAGE OF SCRIPTURE, especially the phrase "he has hid himself among the stuff." I've always wondered why he hid, since Saul seemed to have known he was the elect person. He had already been secretly anointed by Samuel and, therefore, while voting was going on and the lots were being cast, we find here that he hid himself. I don't believe it was out of a wrong motive; otherwise, it would seem to be "fake" humility. This wouldn't fit with the first part of Saul's life, for in his early days and when he was first chosen king, he did seem to be one of the most hopeful persons who could possibly have been called to the office. He had shown great wisdom before this event. I am inclined to believe Saul was being modest in that he concealed himself from honor and from having greatness forced upon him. He had been born great in stature, but now to be made great in office seemed like a burden he did not want to readily sign up for—and so he hid himself among the stuff.

When you think about it, isn't that what we do sometimes? Our place may not seem to be interesting or important in our eyes. We may feel like God passed all kinds of candidates to get to us at the back of the crowd, or maybe you were at the back on purpose and didn't even want to be chosen. Possibly it's something with way too much responsibility, or a task we

33

just don't want. Somehow our heavenly Father in His sovereignty sees something in us we may not ever be able to see in ourselves.

Aren't you glad He takes all the Sauls who are hiding behind the stuff and gives them a new heart? Then He calls the little shepherd boys, all the Davids who are in the field attending the sheep, and anoints them. Thank God, He takes all the Moseses who are on the backside of the desert with nothing to look at but a burning bush, who can't even speak plain. God was merciful to Moses who thought he couldn't move past that obstacle and gave him a Joshua to speak for him. He calls these individuals from places of obscurity and puts them in places they never thought they would be. God does know best, and He does see beyond our fear of failure or feelings of inferiority, and even when we're hiding behind the stuff, He gently calls us for His purposes, not ours.

Oh God, please don't pass us by when we're hiding, or scared, or for whatever reason it may be. Draw us out so we can be of service in Your kingdom.

~Paula

My Bible Reading Plan

☐ Day 43   Numbers 10–12
☐ Day 44   Numbers 13–15
☐ Day 45   Numbers 16–18
☐ Day 46   Numbers 19–21
☐ Day 47   Numbers 22–24
☐ Day 48   Numbers 25–27
☐ Day 49   Numbers 28–30

My Prayer Journal

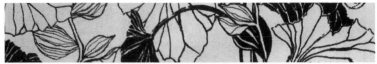

Ecouragement Cookies

*In the multitude of my anxieties within me, Your comforts
delight my soul* (Psalms 94:19 NKJV).

I DECIDED TO FLY FROM CHATTANOOGA to see my newest
grandson, Jaxon, in Detroit. My grandson and granddaughter,
Brayden and Hailey, were on fall break. I knew they would
enjoy the trip, so on the spur-of-the-moment we packed a
bag and left the next day. Did I mention my daughter and
son-in-law also live with my grandson? All the more reason
to go. Hailey is nine, and though excited about flying, she
was a little nervous. As we were walking toward the plane,
she said: "Nana, my heart feels like it has butterflies in it ...
thinking about if we have a wreck and crash. What do planes
crash into, Nana? There's nothing in the sky." I reassured her
it was fine, and we found our seats. Before we ascended, the
flight attendant asked her and Brayden if they wanted some
cookies. You know, those wonderful Biscoff cookies that are
crumbly and almost melt in your mouth. I was not offered
any. I suppose I didn't look nervous enough, or maybe wasn't
young enough. Who knows? Anyway, after this oh-so-kind-
gesture from the very thoughtful flight attendant, Hailey
looked at me and said: "This is the best place ever! She gave
me a cookie." All signs of any jitters were gone. What a trans-
formation of her feelings.

This was a gentle reminder once again of the power of
spoken words and encouragement. Also, a reminder of how
wonderful it is when I feel as if I have butterflies in my heart
as Hailey did, or my palms are sweaty from nervousness, that
I can go to my heavenly Father and His words can soothe and

calm my anxious spirit. I'm reminded of the whimsical story I heard once about a herd of buffalo roaming the range when a tourist passed by. "Those are the mangiest looking beasts I've ever seen," he exclaimed. One buffalo turned to another and said, "I think I just heard a discouraging word!" Even when I'm in a place of excitement or anticipation about my spiritual journey, there are times of questioning about the unseen trials and problems that it could bring, as well. With Hailey, it was as simple as a smile and a cookie. Oh, if it were only that simple in our daily walk. But, we are promised protection from weapons that are forged for our destruction, for a high, strong tower we can run into and find safety, for angels to encamp around us, or for a pillar of fire by night to lead us and a cloud by day, as God provided for the children of Israel. Now that's so much more powerful than a cookie. Praise God!

Oh God, thank You so much for Your presence in my life no matter how apprehensive or scared I may feel. You are my comfort.

~Paula

My Bible Reading Plan

☐	Day 50	Numbers 31–33
☐	Day 51	Numbers 34–36
☐	Day 52	Deuteronomy 1–3
☐	Day 53	Deuteronomy 4–6
☐	Day 54	Deuteronomy 7–9
☐	Day 55	Deuteronomy 10–12
☐	Day 56	Deuteronomy 13–15

My Prayer Journal

Failure Is Not Fatal

Brothers and sisters, I do not consider myself yet to have taken hold of it. But one thing I do: Forgetting what is behind and straining toward what is ahead, I press on toward the goal to win the prize for which God has called me heavenward in Christ Jesus (Philippians 3:13-14 NIV).

IT WOULD BE HARD FOR MOST PEOPLE TO PINPOINT the first moment they felt as though they had failed at parenting. The first two weeks of my son Jaxon's life, I thought I was doing a great job. I never missed a feeding, he was most often content, I was rocking this parenting. Then we went to his checkup. The reality of my perfectly healthy baby was now met with the reality that I had basically been unknowingly starving my son for the first 14 days of his life. When I thought he was getting nourishment from my body, he was barely getting enough to keep weight on his little body. My eight-pound, five-ounce son had lost almost two pounds in just a few short days. Talk about a punch in the gut—to know it was my fault and that my body had failed him. Thank God, it was not life-threatening and all he needed was extra supplement from formula. Hearing those words that we could resolve this brought us much relief, but my mind chalked that up as strike one on the mom "fail board."

If you had me write down every little thing that happened in the first 12 months of his life, I could easily do so. Like the time I panicked when his tear duct was inflamed, and I googled every possible diagnosis, convincing myself he would go blind in the next two hours if I didn't resolve it. Loving this tiny human so much made my heart break quicker and my

mind wander farther in times of distress. It is my job to keep my child safe and even early on, I accepted that duty with full force, determined that failing was not an option.

That word "failure" can be a knife that slowly goes deeper into the heart with each new mistake we make. The Enemy will so quickly use our failures to try and define our identity. As a new mom, I learned it is easy to cling to these failures instead of trusting that it is part of the process. Through each day, I have to decide to push forward and truly forget the things that are behind and reach out for the things ahead. I will never be a perfect mother, wife, daughter, sister, or friend, but I thank God for grace to keep on going, even when my daily failures outweigh my success. Just remember that success is not final, failure is not fatal: it is the courage to continue that counts.

Lord, You know my every thought and intention. I pray
when I feel overtaken by my failures and mistakes that you
remind me of who I truly am. Thank you that it's part of the
process for living the life you have called me to live.

~Tara

My Bible Reading Plan

☐ Day 57   Deuteronomy 16–18
☐ Day 58   Deuteronomy 19–21
☐ Day 59   Deuteronomy 22–24
☐ Day 60   Deuteronomy 25–27
☐ Day 61   Deuteronomy 28–30
☐ Day 62   Deuteronomy 31–34
☐ Day 63   Joshua 1–3

My Prayer Journal

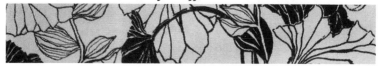

Fear Tactic

Hezekiah received the letter from the messengers and read it.
Then he went up to the temple of the Lord and spread it out
before the Lord. And Hezekiah prayed to the Lord
(2 Kings 19:14-15 NIV).

FOR MANY OF MY DEVOTIONALS and Bible readings, I use the audio portion on my Bible app, so every day I go to whatever plan I'm taking part in and listen to the audio. Today, the reading was in 2 Kings and it was a passage of Scripture I've read many times before. Here's the deal. Sennacherib sent a threatening letter to Hezekiah to ridicule his God and use the scare tactic that God would not be his defender or deliverer. The kings of Assyria were out to get him. This foe was reminding him of the other countries these kings had defeated, so guess what, Hezekiah, you won't be any different. God had other plans. That night the angel of the Lord went into the Assyrian camp and killed 85,000 soldiers. When everyone else awakened the next morning, there were dead bodies lying everywhere. Now that will make the enemy turn around and retreat the quickest way they can to get back from whence they came.

In some strange way, I feel I can relate to this, because I am literal in my prayers and my interaction with God the Father. I talk to Him just like I would talk to my friend sitting beside me on the couch or sitting across from me drinking a cup of coffee, because I know He's a God that takes part in everyday real life. As I was contemplating this passage, I began to think about the ways we ask God to intervene in our lives. My first thought initially was,

well, most people couldn't do what Hezekiah did, because folks just don't send letters that often anymore. In this day of technology, most communication is done through email or texting. What if we took our emails, you know those we get from time-to-time that are so distressing, and perhaps lay our cell phones in front of the Lord and pray about whatever messages we may receive before we react to them? I have, and I found God can read my emails and text messages just as easily as He read Hezekiah's threatening letter. Remember God is the same yesterday, today, and forever. If He delivered Hezekiah from his enemies, we can certainly expect God to intervene in the lives of His children right here and now in our time of need. Thank you, God!

Lord God, You are faithful to hear the cries of distress. I am so thankful to You that when I lay my cause before You, it does not go unanswered.

~Paula

My Bible Reading Plan

☐ Day 64   Joshua 4–6
☐ Day 65   Joshua 7–9
☐ Day 66   Joshua 10–12
☐ Day 67   Joshua 13–15
☐ Day 68   Joshua 16–18
☐ Day 69   Joshua 19–21
☐ Day 70   Joshua 22–24

My Prayer Journal

For My Own Good

So then, it was not you who sent me here, but God. He made me father to Pharaoh, lord of his entire household and ruler of all Egypt (Genesis 45:8 NIV).

I'M NOT FOND OF NEEDLES. Do you remember having to get those injections when you were little, and someone would always say, "This is for your own good." That certainly didn't help me at the time. That needle always looked like you could harpoon a whale with it! But now that I'm older and have used those same words to my children and grandchildren it makes perfect sense. That's why I love this story of Joseph. This is a story of God's faithfulness to get into the middle of bad situations.

I have found myself in a situation or two lately where I have asked the Lord what in the world is this about? My questions normally go like this: Where is this leading? What is going to be the end result? And (I'm sorry), what is the benefit to me and my family when it's all over with? What if it's just a waste of everybody's time? I feel weak to be so honest, but it's hard in my own life when circumstances are forced upon me that were not of my choosing.

Joseph's brothers did an unthinkable wrong by selling him into slavery, but it was God's plan to preserve Joseph's family in a time of great famine. Years later, when it was revealed to them who Joseph was, he assured his brothers that what they meant for evil God meant for good. God knew Joseph needed to be sent to Egypt to save these people and it was all God's plan. How hard would it be for us to realize that many times, whenever

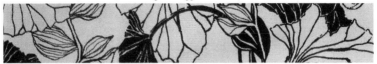

we've been wronged and we've been hurt, it's really going to bring about an end result of what God wanted to do in our lives? We more likely want to say after the fact, this was my own doing and I decided to do it this way, because I knew it would work out, and we don't want to give credit to people who help send us on this journey. That would be like saying they did me wrong and I will not forgive them for what they did to me. How many of us can say with surety that Joseph, who was called the dreamer, could ever have dreamed that one up on his own. After all, why would he ever go to Egypt and how would he even get there? It would've never entered his plans for the future to go to Egypt, because he was a Hebrew, and Scripture tells us Hebrews and Egyptians were not even allowed to sit at the same table and eat together. God had Joseph's future all planned, and He has yours and mine planned, too.

God, I thank you that every plan the devil has for my destruction will only be reworked to come out for my good and Your glory.

~Paula

My Bible Reading Plan

☐ Day 71   Judges 1–3
☐ Day 72   Judges 4–6
☐ Day 73   Judges 7–9
☐ Day 74   Judges 10–12
☐ Day 75   Judges 13–15
☐ Day 76   Judges 16–18
☐ Day 77   Judges 19–21

My Prayer Journal

Glimmer

May the Lord smile on you and be gracious to you
(Numbers 6:25 NLT).

I'M AN OBSERVANT PERSON when it comes to watching expressions on people's faces or their reactions to certain things or situations. I was in church at a funeral in which my husband had a small part. A lot of people were there, a choir was singing, and there were several speakers honoring the life of a special man. As my husband was speaking, I found myself doing what I do quite often, and that was smiling. Having a pleasant look on my face, I felt touched by his words which were honorable and truly heartfelt sentiments toward this dear saint of God. After he was seated, the main speaker arose and walked to the podium. I noticed something. His wife was singing in the choir, and I just happened to be glancing at her as her husband began to speak. Although she had a pleasant look on her face otherwise, when he got up, her face lit up with the most beautiful smile and a gleam was in her eyes that had not been there for any of the other speakers. Of course, I recognized her smile, and I recognized the gleam in her eyes; it was familiar to me, because it was the look of love and the feeling of admiration towards her husband. Although both our husbands expressed wonderful words, I would not have asked her which one she thought had done the best, because I'm certain of what her answer would have been, just as you can be sure of mine.

As I began to think about it, my mind turned toward the thought, *What is there in my life that would make God, my heavenly Father, smile toward me?* Do I represent Him with my words in a way that makes Him smile? Does the way I

48

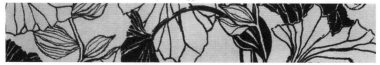

live my life every day put a smile on His face? When I speak words of doubt, unbelief, or fear, does it make Him sad? When I'm frustrated or even angry because things don't go like I think they should, does He frown at my actions? I want not just my words, but everything I do, everything I think, to please my Lord and Savior. None of us are perfect, but if we walk in the light of His perfect love, His light will shine through us. When I think about Him and all He's done for me, I want the glimmer in my eyes toward Him to be seen by others. More importantly, I want there to be a glimmer in His eyes of love and admiration as He looks at me and hears my words spoken to Him and about Him. I don't just want Him to say, "Well done, my good and faithful servant," though I can't imagine any better words than that toward me, but I would like to hear Him say, "Well said, you made Me smile."

Lord, I love You so much, and I'm so thankful that You give me joy that puts a smile on my face no matter what my situation may be. You are wonderful.

~Paula

My Bible Reading Plan

☐ Day 78   Ruth 1–4
☐ Day 79   1 Samuel 1–3
☐ Day 80   1 Samuel 4–6
☐ Day 81   1 Samuel 7–9
☐ Day 82   1 Samuel 10–12
☐ Day 83   1 Samuel 13–15
☐ Day 84   1 Samuel 16–18

My Prayer Journal

He Is Enough

*Cast thy burden upon the Lord, and he shall sustain thee:
he shall never suffer the righteous to be moved
(Psalm 55:22 KJV).*

HAS ANYTHING EVER BEEN SO PRIVATE IN YOUR LIFE, residing so deep inside your being it felt like it pierced even through to your very soul? I'm not talking about sin or wrong in your life, I'm talking about needs maybe within your family or your personal life that are so hurtful and so painful it's hard for you to even verbalize it to God or even speak it out loud? I have to tell you I have been in that place in the past. The Lord reminded me of an incident a few years ago where I was sitting in the midst of about 1,000 ladies at a conference. The speaker had preached such a dynamic, anointed sermon that night, and at the end of the message, there was an altar call given for various needs represented in the congregation. At the time, I remember how desperate my spirit felt with the burden I was carrying, and as the plea was being given for those to come forward for prayer, I felt a deep desperation. I wept, and as tears streamed down my cheeks, I felt so alone even though I was surrounded by countless women who would have been willing to pray with me. On the inside, I remember thinking that not one solitary person in this auditorium knows what I'm going through, and I can't tell them. Even though perhaps I was wrong in my thinking, I did not proceed to the front. I remained in my seat. As I sat there, God spoke to my heart and deep into my spirit. Although I didn't feel like I had

51

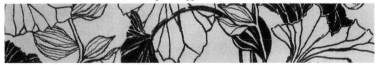

come to the place where I could tell anyone else, I could tell Him and He was enough. A sweet peace flooded over me as I realized that, yes indeed, He is enough.

Maybe right now in your life you're struggling with something more difficult than anything you ever thought you would have to face. Maybe you feel like you could be in a crowd of one million people and be so alone that not one person could understand the way you feel and the burden you are carrying. The Word of God promises me and you that if we will cast all our cares on Him, He will carry them, and He will sustain us through it all. Even when we feel isolated, maybe even misunderstood, hurt, disappointed, or disillusioned, our heavenly Father will be there before, in the middle of, and after we reach the point where we can finally ask others for the help we need. He is our all in all—the all-sufficient One.

God, I am not able to carry my burdens without You, and I'm so thankful You always remind me that I don't have to. Thank you for sustaining me in all my trials. Thank you that when I can't tell anyone, You are sufficient.

~Paula

My Bible Reading Plan

☐ Day 85   1 Samuel 19–21
☐ Day 86   1 Samuel 22–24
☐ Day 87   1 Samuel 25–27
☐ Day 88   1 Samuel 28–31
☐ Day 89   2 Samuel 1–3
☐ Day 90   2 Samuel 4–6
☐ Day 91   2 Samuel 7–9

My Prayer Journal

He Knows the Thoughts

You have searched me, Lord, and you know me. You know when I sit and when I rise; you perceive my thoughts from afar (Psalms 139:1-2 NIV).

I'VE HEARD IT SAID, "MARRIAGE IS LIKE VITAMINS: We supplement each other's minimum daily requirements." I was having a conversation with my husband and we were inquiring of each other's thoughts on a particular subject. We wanted to know if we were in agreement on the matter. He might tell you differently, but most of the time, I can tell you what he's going to say before he says it, or I'll know how he's going respond ahead of time to a particular situation. We've been married 39 years, and I'd say with most couples who have been married a long time, this is not an unusual thing. It comes from being with the person so much that you really know his/her point of view and ideas about most subjects. I realize most likely he's had many thoughts I've never had a clue about. We all know some folks who have totally lived a life of deceitfulness and hidden purposes that nobody really knew what they were thinking until after the fact. Have you ever seen in cartoons how they put those little white thought bubbles above a person's head that tells what one is think-ing? That doesn't actually happen in real life. We've probably all laughed and joked around before when we've made the statement: "They don't have a clue what I'm really thinking right now." Sad to say, there are times we wish someone would know our thoughts, because they are so troubled we don't even know how to share them out loud and we need help.

I'm so glad we have a heavenly Father who knows every thought, every desire, every longing, and every need, no matter how great that need is. He promised to be closer than a mother or father, or a sister or brother. Surely, He knows what we need and what we are going to speak before we speak it. He is a mind reader and the greatest counselor and helper we could ever want or desire. He doesn't judge us because of our innermost thoughts; He just steps in to help get us back to the right way of thinking. He can take the most scattered, mixed-up mind and bring renewing and refreshing.

God, thank You for knowing and caring about what I need. You are my helper and I can run to You when I know my own thoughts are off track and You will help renew and refresh my mind.

~Paula

My Bible Reading Plan

My Prayer Journal

He's There

But let all who take refuge in you be glad; let them ever sing for joy. Spread your protection over them, that those who love your name may rejoice in you (Psalms 5:11 NIV).

MY HUSBAND LOVES MOBSTER MOVIES. No matter how many we watch, it seems there's a common thread prevalent through all them. The mob bosses are pitted against one another, they all break the law, they assassinate their enemies, they pay off some of the law enforcement so they will look the other way, but they always protect "the family." Almost without fail, there will be a dark alley and trash cans will be knocked around and flying everywhere. I could go on, but you get the picture by now.

I'm a visual person, and God speaks to me through everyday common circumstances. Recently, I was thanking God for His faithfulness to meet our needs wherever we are. In my mind, suddenly, I thought about how in almost all those mobster movies I referred to, human resources and intervention can only go so far. I think about scenes where the police are attempting to chase down or apprehend criminals and trying their best to protect the good guys. Then, someone turns and goes down a dark alley and dives behind trashcans where they think no one can see them. It came to me how every time we feel like we are running down a dark alley, are trapped, have nowhere to hide, and, at times, not even any trash cans to dive behind, that God picks up where human resources stop. Whenever we feel like protection from other places is not available any longer and we feel totally and completely vulnerable,

I'm so glad God is there. He follows us, or leads us, down all the dark alleys we feel like we're walking through alone. Behind the stench of all the filth that's been discarded in those trash cans, and even when we are in those dark despondent, smelly places in life, the Father is standing right there beside us reminding us He never leaves us and never forsakes us—"Yea, though I walk through the valley of the shadow of death, Thou art with me, Thy rod and Thy staff they comfort me." Praise God!

Father, thank you that You are waiting for us in all those dark places before we ever get there. You are our source for everything we will ever need.

~Paula

My Bible Reading Plan

☐ Day 99   1 Kings 7–9
☐ Day 100   1 Kings 10–12
☐ Day 101   1 Kings 13–15
☐ Day 102   1 Kings 16–18
☐ Day 103   1 Kings 19–22
☐ Day 104   2 Kings 1–3
☐ Day 105   2 Kings 4–6

My Prayer Journal

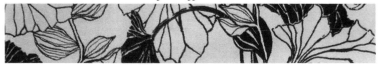

How Much Light?

The unfolding of your words gives light; it gives under-standing to the simple (Psalms 119:130 NIV).

SEVERAL TIMES THROUGH THE YEARS we have lived in our house, we have suffered power outages for different reasons. Sometimes, it's weather-related or outages due to overloads in our area. Sometimes the power is disrupted for reasons of which we are never aware. Like many of you, I have candles and flashlights scattered throughout the house. Although most of my candles are used for fragrance, the flashlights are in case we need to go outside after dark or need to light a space where lighting is insufficient. During the times when we have no electricity, they become a light source inside the house so we don't fall down the stairs or run into walls. We've all heard what a great difference a small candle makes in utter darkness, and how far its light shines; however, I have found if you are in a small room with walls and no outlet into the other rooms, it doesn't do any good if you don't have a candle or a flashlight in each room.

I was thinking about that one day when I was made aware of a wonderful ministry a particular person had, and how they indeed were a great light shining in the darkness in the middle of that ministry calling. After many days of thinking about this, although I rejoiced in it, I began to feel bad about the fact my light seemed so small in comparison to theirs. Was it conviction? I don't think so. I think the answer may lie in the word I used a couple of sentences ago: "comparison." No matter how bad I want to, or how hard I try, I cannot be faithful with what God has given to somebody else. I can't be

faithful with his/her gifts or talents. I can't be the light in their darkness, because God did not put me where He put them. He placed me in the surroundings of my ministry and my calling. God has called me to be the light that shines in the dark places where He has placed me. That is where I must be faithful with all the Father has invested in me. In somebody else's dark place, my light wouldn't shine bright enough, because my flashlight might only work on AAA batteries, while his/hers works on a D battery—that means it's a monster flashlight compared to a screwdriver-size flashlight and it is so much stronger and brighter. In my place where I have been called and equipped with the right size light, my light can dispel the darkness around me. It's up to God to determine the size of the flashlight and the candle. He knows the right size, for the right place, to achieve the right purpose. Yes, He does! Hallelujah!

Oh God, help me not to feel bad or inferior about the light you have placed in my hands. Help me only to be faithful with what You have given to me specifically, for Your purpose to be carried out in me and through me.

~Paula

My Bible Reading Plan

- ☐ Day 106   2 Kings 7–9
- ☐ Day 107   2 Kings 10–12
- ☐ Day 108   2 Kings 13–15
- ☐ Day 109   2 Kings 16–18
- ☐ Day 110   2 Kings 19–21
- ☐ Day 111   2 Kings 22–25
- ☐ Day 112   1 Chronicles 1–3

My Prayer Journal

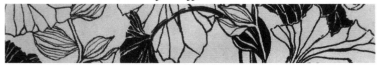

I Can't Do All

I can do all things through Christ who strengthens me
(Philippians 4:13 NKJV).

TOO OFTEN, "I" IS AS BIG AS A MOUNTAIN and seems to be the most powerful letter in the alphabet. It looms over me as deep as an ocean and as vast as a wilderness. Many times, "I" is the biggest obstacle in my walk with God.

One day, as evening was approaching, and the hours of the day were coming to a close, I reflected on the events of the day and realized just how many times, and in how many conversations, the word "I" had been used. Even while writing this devotion, it is difficult to share these thoughts without using that word; "I want," "I need," "I feel," "I think." That's the realization, because this is certain, I cannot overcome my fear of failure, for I can do nothing within the confines of this large, unfathomable obstacle of the flesh that stands in front of me. I am hopelessly lost when left to my own devices. At other times, the opposite is true, and I am certain that I have a plan and I know what to do. Got it all worked out. Piece of cake. "Easy peezy" as my grandkids like to say.

However, there is a truth I'm so glad will always remain, and that is this: God is the Great I Am. It's not me, myself, and I as I hear people jokingly say sometimes. It is Father, Son, and Holy Spirit. I'm not left on my own to figure out and fulfill my own wants, needs, and desires. Yes, I can do a lot of things, because God has enabled me with the gifts and talents I need to do His will and His

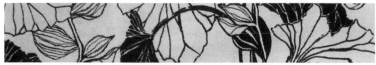

bidding, but I'm so thankful that when that ends, the rest of the story is: "I can do ALL things through Christ who strengthens me." Praise God for that promise.

God, I get weary sometimes of falsely thinking I have to figure out so many things. Help me remember that "I" is not the most important word. YOU are my help.

~Paula

My Bible Reading Plan

☐	Day 113	1 Chronicles 4–6
☐	Day 114	1 Chronicles 7–9
☐	Day 115	1 Chronicles 10–12
☐	Day 116	1 Chronicles 13–15
☐	Day 117	1 Chronicles 16–18
☐	Day 118	1 Chronicles 19–21
☐	Day 119	1 Chronicles 22–24

My Prayer Journal

I Have a Right

Dear children, let us not love with words or speech but with actions and in truth (1 John 3:18 NIV).

I GOT FRUSTRATED WITH SOMEONE I lOVE. The thing that frustrated me that day would not likely have even bothered me much on any other given day. It was so silly you'd probably laugh and say, "Is that all?" I'm not given to emotional outbursts. It's not my nature or my character; however, on this particular day, I felt I deserved the right to express my feelings. I usually try to remain silent until I can talk about a situation with a clear mind, but that day I exercised my free will to voice my opinion. I said things I didn't mean, and things I instantly wanted to retract, but I couldn't. I looked at my husband (Oops, I told, didn't I?) and the look of surprise on his face was evident. My feeling in that moment, after the words were said and it was too late to take them back, was instant regret. Immediate words of sorrow and anguish began to gush forth from the same mouth that was previously spewing my "right to speak" words just moments before. I felt sick to my stomach, instant sadness lodged in my being, and tears at the surface of my eyes were waiting to spill over. I knew I would spend days with these dreadful feelings of trying to forgive myself and praying I truly was forgiven. Of course, I was forgiven, and we even laughed about it later, but the struggle within my own self lasted a while.

I heard someone say, "You never know whose eyes God is watching you out of." Now that's a sobering thought. So, here's the big question in my mind: "What does my heavenly Father think of me when I act like that?" As a child, I was

often reminded God sees even if no one else does, but unfortunately most of the time someone else does see. I don't want the Father to be ashamed of me and my actions. I want to represent Him well.

It's thought provoking, I know. Absolutely, most assuredly, we will all have times of frustration, but if we can try to think a few minutes ahead of our momentary emotions to what the outcome may be, perhaps we would choose to give up our "rights." Our harsh words may not greatly affect our relationship with the other person, but it's no fun to deal with the after effects of what it does to the inside of the person who exercises one's right to free speech. I hope you will be reminded to constantly pray for awareness beforehand, as I try to do. Before a situation spirals out of control, remember God indeed will be watching through another set of eyes—eyes looking toward you, not eyes looking through you at someone else.

God, please remind me that my "rights" are wrong when
it wounds another person. Give me Your wisdom in these
situations I pray.

~Paula

My Bible Reading Plan

☐   Day 120   1 Chronicles 25–27
☐   Day 121   1 Chronicles 28–29
☐   Day 122   2 Chronicles 1–3
☐   Day 123   2 Chronicles 4–6
☐   Day 124   2 Chronicles 7–9
☐   Day 125   2 Chronicles 10–12
☐   Day 126   2 Chronicles 13–15

My Prayer Journal

I'll Catch You

Even to your old age and gray hairs I am he, I am he who will sustain you. I have made you and I will carry you; I will sustain you and I will rescue you (Isaiah 46:4 NIV).

I HAD A DREAM NOT VERY LONG AGO. The subject of this dream was my mother-in-law, who came and spent about five months with us. We were always reinforcing the fact she didn't ever need to go down the stairs alone, because she can't see too well, and she could easily miss a step or lose her footing and fall. She was very understanding about our concerns and made peace with our wishes. I'm sure with this always on my mind, it was the reason for my dream. I didn't perceive this to be anything spiritual, it was just one of those things you chuckle about and then forget over time. But in this dream, I was coming from downstairs headed upstairs to the bedroom. Our stairs go up a little way, then there's a landing, and they turn and go up quite a few more steps. As I got to the landing, I saw my mother-in-law coming down the stairs and I could tell she was not going to make it. She kept sinking lower and lower as she was walking, until finally her legs collapsed underneath her and she rolled the last four steps downward. I sat down and caught her, and she's laying in my lap, leaning against me. I asked her if she was all right and she replied yes. I said well, okay. We'll sit here, you can lean against me until you feel strong enough to stand up and walk, and then we will get up. Then I awoke. I went to her bedroom to share the dream with her and we both got a good laugh out of it. Did I tell you she's 89 years old? She replied, "Boy, that would be a mess, wouldn't it?"

As I thought about that throughout the day, I was reminded of what an exact scenario it is in the life of a Christian when it comes to the relationship we have in Christ Jesus. It's exactly what I feel happens to me so many times, more often than I could even share. Frequently, I start out feeling strong and able to make the journey, and then as I go, my spiritual legs seem to get weaker and weaker with each step. Finally, I realize I can't make it and I feel myself collapse. At that point, I wonder how bad I'm going to be hurt when I land at the bottom. You know what? Every single time, without fail, I roll into the arms of Jesus and He says, "You're going to be okay, because I'm going to hold you and comfort you until you're strong enough to stand back up and finish your journey." Now that I reflect on it, maybe it was a spiritual dream after all. Sounds like it, doesn't it?

Father, I thank You that every time my knees get weak and buckle underneath me, You are waiting to catch me. You never fail to be there.

~Paula

My Bible Reading Plan

☐	Day 127	2 Chronicles 16–18
☐	Day 128	2 Chronicles 19–21
☐	Day 129	2 Chronicles 22–24
☐	Day 130	2 Chronicles 25–27
☐	Day 131	2 Chronicles 28–30
☐	Day 132	2 Chronicles 31–33
☐	Day 133	2 Chronicles 34–36

My Prayer Journal

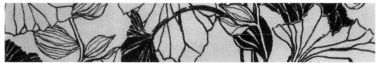

Impossible Territory

The Lord is close to the brokenhearted and saves those who are crushed in spirit (Psalm 34:18 NIV).

SOMETHING SAID ONE DAY TRIGGERED A MEMORY from my childhood, and I'll venture to say many reading this will remember it as well: "Where no man has gone before." Remember?

"Where no man has gone before" is a phrase made popular through its use in the title sequence of the original Star Trek science fiction television series, describing the mission of the starship Enterprise. The complete introductory speech, spoken by William Shatner at the beginning of each episode, is: "Space: The Final Frontier. These are the voyages of the starship Enterprise. Its five-year mission: to explore strange new worlds, to seek out new life and new civilizations, to boldly go where no man has gone before." Does this bring back memories to anyone else? It does if you are like me and of a certain age (which I shall not pursue any further).

As I pondered that thought, I also began to think about other places humanity can never have access to, but God does. What about matters of the heart and mind that are unreachable? You can find the most renowned and well-acclaimed physicians known to mankind, who have degrees and accomplishments as long as your arm, that can go inside the heart and unclog arteries that are a pending death sentence. They can even replace a worn-out heart with a different heart. Who could have ever imagined? But, the invisible things inside a heart, those are an entirely different matter. A good doctor can cut out a cancerous tumor if conditions

are right, but he cannot open the brain or a heart and excise a hurt or the pain of unforgiveness. He can't take out hatred or sin or take a broken heart and stitch it back together with healing sutures. A doctor cannot remove and help heal a memory that caused unthinkable hurt or trauma. He can't see the physical evidence of those conditions. How wonderful it would be if he could. Can you imagine how long the waiting list of patients would be for a surgical procedure to correct heartbreak or to heal a painful memory? How excited it makes me feel to know there's a man named Jesus who can do exactly that very thing. Praise God, He can go into unknown territory where no man has ever gone before. He doesn't have a waiting list, you can have immediate access to emergency care. Hallelujah! Turn it over to Him.

Oh, my Father, thank You for being my Great Physician,
who goes beyond the boundaries of the physical
into all the impossible places in my life.

~Paula

My Bible Reading Plan

☐ Day 134   Ezra 1–3
☐ Day 135   Ezra 4–6
☐ Day 136   Ezra 7–10
☐ Day 137   Nehemiah 1–3
☐ Day 138   Nehemiah 4–6
☐ Day 139   Nehemiah 7–9
☐ Day 140   Nehemiah 10–13

My Prayer Journal

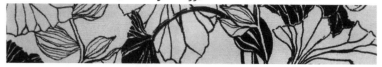

In the Shelter

For in the time of trouble He shall hide me in His pavilion; In the secret place of His tabernacle He shall hide me; He shall set me high upon a rock (Psalm 27:5 NKJV).

LOTS OF THINGS HAPPEN WHEN YOU START GETTING OLDER. I won't go into them here, the list would be way too long. One thing that happens with me is when I'm going through struggles, my mind goes back frequently to songs I heard in church when I was growing up. I and the good Lord have always had this thing where He reminds me of those songs, and when I'm faced with trials I can't seem to talk myself through, I will remember one of those songs from years past. When that happens, I just sing and sing until it alters my thinking pattern. Today, here is my song: *When the world all around me is raging, and it's filled with many alarms, trust in Jesus and He will keep you in the shelter of His arms. There is peace in the time of struggle. There is peace in the midst of the storm. There is peace though the world be raging. In the shelter of His arms.*

What's raging in your life today? Is it struggles with children, aging parents, extended family? Maybe it's a personal struggle no one sees or even knows about but you. There are times when it's not even personal struggles, but when the world around us seems to have gone into convulsions. We can't make sense of anything and we wonder where God is in all of it. Rest assured, it's during those times He will wrap you in

His arms, give you calm assurance, and He will be your shelter.

God, I thank you that Your arms are open wide and I can
run and find shelter from all the storms and
all the struggles that may come my way.

~Paula

My Bible Reading Plan

☐ Day 141   Esther 1–3
☐ Day 142   Esther 4–6
☐ Day 143   Esther 7–10
☐ Day 144   Job 1–3
☐ Day 145   Job 4–6
☐ Day 146   Job 7–9
☐ Day 147   Job 10–12

My Prayer Journal

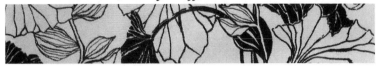

Maybe I Should Have Stayed in Bed

Your eyes saw my unformed body; all the days ordained for me were written in your book before one of them came to be (Psalms 139:16 NIV).

IT WAS THAT KIND OF A DAY when you know everything you do will seem to go wrong. I'm usually comfortable with the normal routine of my day, but sometimes there is just an unsettledness that overshadows everything else. Do you ever have those crazy days? Maybe it's staring at your clothes hanging in the closet and not being able to decide what to wear for the day. Some days, I just don't like the way my clothes feel, and those days usually mean I will be hanging clothes back on hangers for twenty minutes before I finally find something that suits my mood. Or, have you ever walked into the kitchen and just stood there, because nothing sounds good to eat, or you just don't know if you want to go buy groceries today or wait until tomorrow. Can I be honest and tell you, I have great difficulty dealing with those days. Suffice it to say, it's an "I should have stayed in bed kind of day."

I try to take advantage of those times to pray and read my Bible. Why not? If I determine my brain is out of gear for the day, I often find myself being drawn into His presence. Perhaps this may be the reason I land here from time to time. As I read this passage of scripture in Psalms 139, I'm reminded of the power of the truth. Many of you are familiar with these words, but maybe you, like me, need a reminder. When I got to verse 16, the realization hit me again. It's like this—even on this kind of day, just

as with more decisive, productive ones—it was already written in His book before I was ever born. It was ordained already before it ever dawned. Surely, if God knew before I was born the number of hairs that would be on my head, He's not unaware of this. And, if He knew that, He knew how many heartbeats I would have, He knew how many breaths I would take, He knew the number of my days, and He knew the content of my days ahead of time. Most assuredly, we don't need to feel useless and worthless to God on a day like that. There are times we just need to be still and remember we are in His plan. He holds us secure in the palm of His hand, and we are still of benefit to God. Take the time to be still and listen to His feelings, not yours.

God, I am personally valuable to You. Thank You that You accept me because You know me. I choose to listen to Your voice in the emptiness of my own surroundings and feelings.

~Paula

My Bible Reading Plan

☐	Day 148	Job 13–15
☐	Day 149	Job 16–18
☐	Day 150	Job 19–21
☐	Day 151	Job 22–24
☐	Day 152	Job 25–27
☐	Day 153	Job 28–30
☐	Day 154	Job 31–33

My Prayer Journal

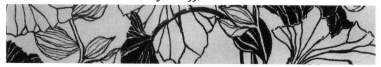

My Every Day

Rejoice always, pray continually, give thanks in all circumstances; for this is God's will for you in Christ Jesus (1 Thessalonians 5:16-18 NIV).

WHEN I WAS YOUNGER, I WAS BOUND BY THINKING GOD was so holy (and He is holy) that I had to meet with Him only in those sacred, dedicated places of prayer I had established for our meetings. You know, that place of beautiful, peaceful intercession that is portrayed most of the time. At that time in my life, there were some hindrances in the form of three little future women of God. Oh yes, go ahead and throw a puppy into that scenario, as well. I'm going to invent a new word here, *hecticness*. I could never find the perfect time to pray. Here's how it went most of the time: I would go to the living room to my prayer chair and begin to pray. Inevitably, I would be disrupted by quarrels over a toy, or the television suddenly turned to an alarming volume. Immediately I would switch from "prayer mode" to "Mommy mode." I would yell, "Turn that down and stop fighting over that toy." Back to prayer mode, "Oh God, You are so good." It was the spiritual version of Jekyll and Hyde. Funny, not funny. It is funny now, as I tell about it, but then it was so frustrating!

What finally happened? My eyes were opened to the real truth. I discovered I didn't have to go to a special, perfect location or wait for a certain time slot to meet with God. It was wonderful when it did work out that way, but it wasn't often. Somehow, God let me know He was right

in the middle of my every day. My everyday schedule, my everyday running to the grocery store, my everyday do-ing laundry and being chauffeur to my kids, my everyday cleaning my house. Those little girls are grown and on their own now, but some of the most awesome prayer and praise meetings I have are still when I'm in my car. I always keep tissues at hand, and I get some strange looks from other drivers passing by, but I don't really care. If I'm in a dressing room, or in a quiet corner, He shows up right in the middle of my "every day." Liberating, to say the least.

God, I sense Your presence anywhere and anytime I speak Your name. Oh, how I thank You for that honor and privilege. Hallelujah!

~Paula

My Bible Reading Plan

My Prayer Journal

Not in Vain

Therefore, my beloved brethren, be steadfast, immovable, always abounding in the work of the Lord, knowing that your labor is not in vain in the Lord
(1 Corinthians 15:58 NKJV).

PART OF AN OLD SONG RESURFACED IN MY MEMORY a few years ago: "Then my living will not be in vain." At the home-going of my stepmom of 24 years, I was reminded of this song. To my knowledge, this precious saint of God never stood behind a pulpit to preach a sermon, but her life spoke more than volumes of sermon books. Her life was not perfect, but it didn't need to be, because God who lived in her and shone through her WAS perfect. I realized all over again that is what really matters. In this life, we can never achieve all we would like to achieve, or dream of achieving, but that's okay as long as our "living" is not in vain.

Growing up, I heard this expression used quite often: "They are too heavenly-minded to be any earthly good." Quite honestly, it referenced the perception of a person who believed themselves to be "very" spiritual who would make those on a lesser plain of spiritual matters feel guilty about something. I suppose it helped to categorize such individuals to ease the mind. I'd like to be able to say I'm spiritually-minded all the time, but unfortunately, as much as I would love to live in a spiritual bubble, I can't. I can't live with my head in the heavens while my fleshly body is still walking around on earth. I ask the heavenly Father to give me joy for the journey, a

song in my heart when it aches from lack of understanding, a spring in my step when I don't feel like walking forward, a confident trust in who HE is and in HIS ability, and to live in and shine forth through me. Through all my imperfections, all my weaknesses, and even at times my doubts and confusion, somehow let it glorify God so I can declare, "My living has not been in vain."

Lord, let my living exemplify You even in the midst of all my imperfections, all my inadequacies, all my faults, and even my failures. Let my life count for You.

~Paula

My Bible Reading Plan

☐ Day 162   Psalms 32–37
☐ Day 163   Psalms 38–44
☐ Day 164   Psalms 45–51
☐ Day 165   Psalms 52–59
☐ Day 166   Psalms 60–67
☐ Day 167   Psalms 68–71
☐ Day 168   Psalms 72–77

My Prayer Journal

Oh, Yes, It Matters

And whatever you do, do it heartily, as to the Lord and not to men, knowing that from the Lord you will receive the reward of the inheritance; for you serve the Lord Christ (Colossians 3:23-24 NKJV).

DOES WHAT WE DO REALLY MAKE A DIFFERENCE? If we live a humble life, if not many people ever know our names, if we never travel to exotic places, if our names are never recognized for anything, does it really matter? One of the people who had great influence in my life is my mother-in-law. She was the one who was known for cooking meatloaf, beans and cornbread, and banana pudding. She was the one who sat on the pew and prayed while her husband preached in the pulpit. She was uncomfortable if called upon to get up in front of people. She was always in the background. Yet, she would come every summer and stay with our children so I could travel with my husband, stand up before people and minister, and go places I would never have been able to take my children. I would have stayed home and missed ministering to a pastor's wife who was distraught, because her child had turned away from God. I would have never had the privilege of praying with a precious sister on the mission field. I wouldn't have seen hundreds rush to an altar in response to an invitation for salvation or watched the Holy Spirit fall on thousands as they worshipped God.

People like my mother-in-law are the unsung heroes. She stepped in to take care of the most precious gifts I have by staying home with our girls so we could fulfill the call of God on our lives. Her sacrifice to do that was as important as her

intercession for her husband when he was in the pulpit. Both selfless acts allowed someone else to do what they were called to do. When I am reminded of the souls we have seen come to Jesus in our travels, I know her part in that harvest is as significant as ours. She made a difference to thousands of men and women who will never know her name. But Jesus knows her, and many like her who don't need a microphone or a platform to be effective for the Kingdom.

Be a hero of the faith. You don't have to have the spotlight to do great things for God. He's looking for some moms and daughters and sisters and grannies to do exploits for Him without ever leaving their homes. Find your prayer closet. Cook a meal for a sick neighbor. Be Jesus with skin on to someone who needs you in your family. God is waiting to use you to make a difference, even if no one else ever sees.

Father, help me recognize the importance of being a servant to others as I serve You. I want to be exactly where You want me to be, doing exactly what You want me to do. I know only then can I find true fulfillment in Your plan for me.

~Paula

My Bible Reading Plan

☐ Day 169   Psalms 78–81
☐ Day 170   Psalms 82–89
☐ Day 171   Psalms 90–97
☐ Day 172   Psalms 98–104
☐ Day 173   Psalms 105–110
☐ Day 174   Psalms 111–118
☐ Day 175   Psalms 119

My Prayer Journal

Pay Attention

*Therefore we must give the more earnest heed to the things
we have heard, lest we drift away* (Hebrews 2:1 NKJV).

MY GRANDDAUGHTER WAS IN A DANCE COMPETITION,
which was exciting because it was her first solo perfor-
mance. She's been in many competitions, but always with
her team. I couldn't go, but I was prepared to watch it
livestream. I had my iPad set up and my phone ready to
record it from that screen. I anxiously kept asking by text,
"When does she dance?" Four more, three more. I decided to go to a better spot with less glare. I had time—I
thought. I got settled and one after another kept entering
and exiting the stage and I didn't see her. Finally, I asked,
and my daughter texted back, "She's already gone. Did
you miss it?" How could I have missed it? I was right there.
I'm sorry to sound childish, but the disappointment was
so overwhelming I started crying. I felt just awful about
myself. The rest of the story is later that night I found out
there were four different competitions simultaneously in
different cities and I was watching Baton Rouge instead
of Nashville. Boy, did I feel better about the fact I didn't
overlook something which was right in front of me, but
did I ever feel stupid over the way I reacted on the same
level as I felt relief.

If you've read my other devotional books, you know already most of the devotions come from life experiences
of which I'm embarrassed sometimes, but I believe we
all have plenty of those moments. As I lay in bed thinking about it that night, I realized all too often that's what

happens when we follow our own plan instead of paying attention to what God is doing. We think we have it figured out, so we prepare and get in place only to discover we have not switched to the right station or setting. Some things are easy enough to figure out on our own, right? Seems like that would be the case, doesn't it? We prepare ourselves, watch and wait, and suddenly we realize somehow we missed it. How in the world could we miss something right in front of our eyes? It's easier to do than we would like to admit. We get so focused on the adjustment of the screen and the location where we are recording, so to speak, that we don't even realize we are on the wrong channel. Next time, I guarantee you I will check for the right location before I get set up for the rest of the process.

Lord, help me not to get so distracted each day by the details of my life that I let what and where You are in my process pass me by.

~Paula

My Bible Reading Plan

☐ Day 176   Psalms 120–127
☐ Day 177   Psalms 128–136
☐ Day 178   Psalms 137–142
☐ Day 179   Psalms 143–150
☐ Day 180   Proverbs 1–3
☐ Day 181   Proverbs 4–6
☐ Day 182   Proverbs 7–9

My Prayer Journal

Pillow Fight

O God, You are my God; Early will I seek You; My soul thirsts for You; My flesh longs for You in a dry and thirsty land where there is no water (Psalm 63:1 NKJV).

SOME MORNINGS I WAKE UP BEFORE DAYLIGHT with the feeling that I need to get up and pray. It's a struggle between wanting to stay under those warm, cozy covers on cold mornings or go to that freezing closet and start praying even before the space heater has time to do its magic. As I lay in bed one morning struggling with my flesh, I could almost picture the devil gathering all his forces for the day and saying: "Okay, it's about time for all those prayer warriors, those wives, moms, and grandmas to get up and start praying over their day and praying over their families, for protection over their grandchildren and committing their lives anew to their Father's plan, giving God total control over circumstances and their situations. It's bad news, boys, so we need to get a head start on it. We all know if they get up saying "Jesus," we are done for. There's so much power in that name we need to do all we can to discourage them so they can't focus on that. We need to make that bed feel so good they can't drag themselves out of it. We want to do all we can do to be a hindrance. If we can get a jump on it and keep them lying there, it's going to make our job a lot easier." As I thought about that, I quickly got up out of bed and as my feet hit the floor, in my mind I could hear one of the demons say, "Oh no, Paula's up. Man the battle stations. Watch out, take cover. Incoming, incoming."

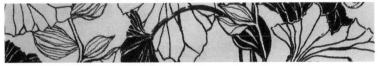

I'd like to believe it's what goes on. I kind of think it does. So, next time you are deciding if your pillow is going to keep you from your prayer closet, just remember our Enemy is hoping he is victorious in the pillow fight!

Lord, I want to be a threat to the Enemy's camp. So, keep speaking and I'll keep doing my part to obey. I want to be used by You to invade the darkness.

~Paula

My Bible Reading Plan

☐ Day 183   Proverbs 10–12
☐ Day 184   Proverbs 13–15
☐ Day 185   Proverbs 16–18
☐ Day 186   Proverbs 19–21
☐ Day 187   Proverbs 22–24
☐ Day 188   Proverbs 25–27
☐ Day 189   Proverbs 28–31

My Prayer Journal

Back Off, Devil!

When the enemy comes in like a flood, the Spirit of the Lord will lift up a standard against him (Isaiah 59:19 NKJV).

Have you ever been so mad at a situation from the Enemy that you literally stomped your foot at the devil? I'm not talking about the scenario I heard about where a lady bought a dress she didn't need. When she got home and her husband questioned her about it, she replied, "The devil made me do it." He asked why she didn't say, "Satan, get thee behind me," as the Bible says to do. She answered, "I did, and he said, it looks good from back here, too." Some circumstances we blame on the devil when actually it's that we're just not following through with the decision we know is the right one to choose.

I was headed for some much-needed time to be still and freshen my listening and waiting skills concerning my spiritual state of being at the time. Only hours before, the enemy of my soul—the devil, the deceitful one, the liar, the thief of all good godly things, just to name a few descriptions—attacked my mind with a vengeance. A strong feeling of being totally and completely overwhelmed, as well as fearful, settled over my spirit. I extended a plea to some closest to me, whom I knew would pray for me, and they prayed. Hour-by-hour, God began to bring me victory.

As I was going down the escalator in the airport the next morning, I stomped my foot, and I stomped it hard. Under my breath, I let the Enemy know in very certain

terms that I absolutely was not letting him get away with this latest tactical effort.

I've come to know these attacks are real, and they always come before a point of some kind of breakthrough in my life. I did get through and gained victory. So can you.

Lord, I thank You that you are my helper, and You are near me when the Enemy attacks, to bring me to complete victory.

~Paula

My Bible Reading Plan

☐ Day 190   Ecclesiastes 1–3
☐ Day 191   Ecclesiastes 4–6
☐ Day 192   Ecclesiastes 7–9
☐ Day 193   Ecclesiastes 10–12
☐ Day 194   Song of Solomon 1–3
☐ Day 195   Song of Solomon 4–6
☐ Day 196   Song of Solomon 7–8

My Prayer Journal

Rain, Rain, Go Away

... and sendeth rain on the just and on the unjust
(Matthew 5:45 NKJV).

MOST OF MY WRITING COMES FROM PERSONAL EX-
PERIENCE. Here's a new experience, because right this
moment in time, I am sitting inside watching the rain.
The problem is that I'm on vacation, and second, I'm at
a nice resort where I've rented a cabana for the day and
it's a washout. Let's compound it even more, because I
set aside two whole days of this week to find a still, quiet
place to finish this book. Well, what do you do? I have no
control over the weather and neither does anyone else.
I've gotten inspiration for a devotion as I sit here watching a Clint Eastwood western in my hotel room, and
that's just not right, because it sounds like a Saturday at
my house on my couch sometimes.

What happens when it rains in your life spiritually?
Occasionally, there are bright sunshiny skies, and then
clouds begin to roll in above your head and the raindrops
start to fall. Maybe it starts out as a drizzle, but then turns
into a gully-washer as we used to say in Texas. Every so
often, storms come with gusty winds that seem to do destruction to our spiritual lives, just like what occurs in
the natural realm. We are forced to change or even cancel
plans, and the devastation seems to take forever to clean
up. Remember this one thing—God still brings the same
good into our lives whether it comes after the storm or
in the sunshine. After all, I'm still and I'm quiet and that's

99

what I wanted, isn't it? I'm just on the inside looking outside instead of the other way around like I had planned. An end always comes to the rain, and many times a most beautiful rainbow will appear on the horizon. It's just called "life," folks! And He's in the middle of it all if we allow Him to be.

God, I thank You that even when it rains, You still allow
me to have the same outcome, so I trust You with the
circumstances.

~Paula

My Bible Reading Plan

☐   Day 197   Isaiah 1–3
☐   Day 198   Isaiah 4–6
☐   Day 199   Isaiah 7–9
☐   Day 200   Isaiah 10–12
☐   Day 201   Isaiah 13–15
☐   Day 202   Isaiah 16–18
☐   Day 203   Isaiah 19–21

My Prayer Journal

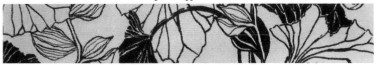

Repurposed Words

Let the words of my mouth and the meditation of my heart be acceptable in Your sight, O Lord, my strength and my Redeemer (Psalm 19:14 NKJV).

I LIKE THE WORD "REPURPOSE." It's easy to figure out the definition because it's exactly what it says. Webster's states the prefix "re" means "again" or "anew." Therefore, something that had a purpose can be used again and assigned a new purpose. I love to take things and give them a new purpose. A few years ago, my daughter lived in a house with a kitchen that had minimal storage space and few cabinets. Right next to the kitchen was a huge coat closet. We asked each other which was more important, a place for coats or for food? Guess what we decided? (Did I mention she has three children?) Right! You got it. We made a trip to Home Depot and by nightfall she had a more than ample food pantry. That coat closet had a new, more efficient purpose. Think about this, if you will. The words that proceed forth from our mouths are powerful. You could write a devotion book every day from now until eternity and the subject of our words could be the main opening page in all of them. Is that because our words have the potential to be the most prosperous tool to build up or the most destructive tool to tear down and destroy? Words have so many lives and so many purposes—maybe more than anything else ever on the face of the earth.

Do I want my words to be encouraging words or destructive words? Oh, there are times I can use words to prove a point by putting a mask on those words to convince myself

and try to convince others they are "wisdom" words. After all, don't we all know someone has to be brave enough to speak the truth? Our words can be masked as: "Constructive criticism," "The right to know," "It's to help them learn," "It will help them toughen up."

Here's a good one: "I had to learn how hard life is, and they need to know to. Everyone's afraid to tell them the truth, so someone has to."

It could go on and on and on. But what if we chose to repurpose our words from cursing to blessing? From speaking death to speaking life? From tearing down to building up? I can't even imagine how much stronger we would be spiritually and in every other way.

What do you choose? Purpose or repurpose?

Father, I'm guilty, plain and simple. Forgive me. I want all I say and do to be pleasing to You. Thank you for reminding me today of this truth.

~Paula

My Bible Reading Plan

☐ Day 204   Isaiah 22–24
☐ Day 205   Isaiah 25–27
☐ Day 206   Isaiah 28–30
☐ Day 207   Isaiah 31–33
☐ Day 208   Isaiah 34–36
☐ Day 209   Isaiah 37–39
☐ Day 210   Isaiah 40–42

My Prayer Journal

Right Fit

For My thoughts are not your thoughts, nor are your ways My ways, says the Lord. For as the heavens are higher than the earth, so are My ways higher than your ways, and My thoughts than your thoughts (Isaiah 55:8-9 NKJV).

I WAS TRYING TO PUT SOME THINGS AWAY IN THE KITCHEN CABINETS. I had removed something wedged in there. I was trying to get it back in and there was no way it was going to fit. I don't know how I got it in there in the first place. The deal is, the upper cabinets hold items I don't use much so when I put them there, I twist and turn them until every square inch is filled. The only problem is when you take them out, you can never quite seem to get them back into the space the same way they were before.

The next morning, the Holy Spirit brought a picture to my mind as I was praying. I was reminded how the night before I'd been trying to cram something into the cabinet where it wouldn't fit. I could see in my mind a big stock pot. I was trying to cram it into this little cabinet where the cups and the glasses were, and outside of tearing that cabinet apart, there was no possible way I was going to be able to make it fit. I was reminded of how we spend so much time trying to create spaces for ourselves that God never intended. We try to cram and squeeze into the places already full of other things and there's no room for us. It's another example of trying to function outside the gifting Christ has called us to walk in. We work so hard to chase down opportunities to get ourselves in places which appear to be "our kind of place," where we just know we

could flourish and be effective. In actuality, we need to step back and remember God created us for a purpose, and the only way to be fulfilled is to recognize and come to terms with the fact the only place of true satisfaction is in the place where God calls us. Don't try to kick down doors that look in the natural as perfect. Do you remember the show "Let's Make a Deal" where you had a choice between door number one, number two, or number three? Each contestant hoped they would pick the door that had the grand prize behind it and not the clunker of a deal. That's the way we view God's gift sometimes—as the "clunker"—the thing we absolutely would not pick if given the choice.

I pray we can each one be at peace by trusting God's design to know where we fit and where we don't fit. That's the best deal.

Father, please help me remember that You are the one who knows the details of what and where my life needs to go. I trust you with it!

~Paula

My Bible Reading Plan

☐ Day 211   Isaiah 43–45
☐ Day 212   Isaiah 46–48
☐ Day 213   Isaiah 49–51
☐ Day 214   Isaiah 52–54
☐ Day 215   Isaiah 55–57
☐ Day 216   Isaiah 58–60
☐ Day 217   Isaiah 61–63

My Prayer Journal

Scary

When I am afraid, I put my trust in you (Psalm 56:3 NIV).

LIFE IS FULL OF SCARY. There you are. Bottom line. Scary leads to paranoia. Panic. Fear. Palpitations. Sleeplessness. Anxiety. That's just to name a few things. Why do I tell you this? Those around me know I tell on myself constantly. I always say, "I'm never going to tell anyone I did something that dumb." Alas, I just can't help myself. Guess I feel like other folks do dumb stuff, too, and just aren't shameless enough to tell it. Oh, well. Case in point. Right now, we are in the middle of flu season and everywhere I turn I hear about someone dying. It's heart wrenching, to say the least. Not only that, but it seems like tragedy is always looming whether in news stories on television, or social media on our phones or computers, or documentaries on television, or just plain old word-of-mouth. And it definitely, as it should, drives us to our knees in prayer.

That being said, I recently became so fearful one evening about these things that I told my husband I felt like I was smothering and feeling somewhat panicked. After assessment of my current situation, I knew I had to get hold of my emotional state of being and do something. I'm sure you've heard the phrase, "stop, drop, and roll." I knew I had to stop, look up, and sing. I began to sing all the songs I knew about peace and about God's faithfulness. I was in the kitchen cooking dinner and I just kept on working and singing in the middle of clanging pots and pans. I began to feel the soothing presence of the Holy Spirit, and my husband, who was sitting in the

den, called out and said, "Are you singing your way to victory?" I was definitely doing just that.

I had to remind myself God is greater! He gives me and you the power to live courageously, boldly, and fearlessly in this life even when everything that surrounds us tells us life is full of "scary." His truth whispers strong and sure to the very depths of our spirits. So, all that stuff on your mind?

Give it to Him—again, and sleep in peace tonight.

Father, I choose to replace all my fearful thoughts with
Your words of truth. You know what concerns me;
You've got me covered.

~Paula

My Bible Reading Plan

☐ Day 218   Isaiah 64–66
☐ Day 219   Jeremiah 1–3
☐ Day 220   Jeremiah 4–6
☐ Day 221   Jeremiah 7–9
☐ Day 222   Jeremiah 10–12
☐ Day 223   Jeremiah 13–15
☐ Day 224   Jeremiah 16–18

My Prayer Journal

Stay Attached

*He alone is my rock and my salvation, my fortress where
I will never be shaken* (Psalms 62:2 NLT).

THE OUTSIDE OF OUR HOME WAS ALWAYS SURROUND-
ED BY BEAUTIFUL ROSES and several different types of
flowers. My mother had a love of these things. I'm not
sure if that's where my love of them began, but I get such
enjoyment from sitting in my sunroom and looking at
the flowers I have in my backyard and those lining both
sides of the driveway going down to the backyard. I have
some that grow tall, probably around three to four feet
in height and are big, round, and gorgeous. The first year
they bloomed and grew, I didn't realize I needed to attach them to stakes in the ground to stabilize them. One
afternoon I came home to find beautiful flowers whose
stems had been bent at the base, lying every which direction on the ground. A strong wind blew that afternoon
and the wind won the battle. I was so disappointed I
could've cried. Actually, I believe I did shed a few tears,
and although I propped them up and secured them, they
remained wilted for the rest of the summer. My flowers
never quite recovered.

Do you realize that's the way it is with our spiritual
lives? We may have so many beautiful, wonderful things
happening in our lives, and oh, how we enjoy those good
times of blessing and fruitfulness. However, no matter
what we do, we must attach ourselves to something. We
must have an anchor, a strong foundation for all we have
done and all we will ever accomplish in and through

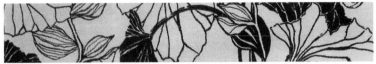

Christ. That way, when the winds blow in and the storm does come our way, we have something that won't let us fall. We can figure out a lot of things on our own, because of experience and learned wisdom from living life. When we get too secure in what we can do for ourselves, we forget that no matter how tall we stand, it only takes one strong, prolonged gust of wind to bend us from our foundation. And like my flowers, though we don't completely break off, we don't recover quickly either. We may remain wilted for quite some time. Certainly, our good Father helps us and we don't stay that way. How wonderful it would be if the beauty were never disturbed in the first place. Be sure you are secured in Him, and then let the winds blow.

Dear God, I need You. Help me stand strong and secure in You, knowing you will keep me when I can't predict the winds of life.

~Paula

My Bible Reading Plan

☐ Day 225   Jeremiah 19–21
☐ Day 226   Jeremiah 22–24
☐ Day 227   Jeremiah 25–27
☐ Day 228   Jeremiah 28–30
☐ Day 229   Jeremiah 31–33
☐ Day 230   Jeremiah 34–36
☐ Day 231   Jeremiah 37–39

My Prayer Journal

Straight and Narrow

But small is the gate and narrow the road that leads to life, and only a few find it (Matthew 7:14 NIV).

WE LIVE IN A NEIGHBORHOOD WITH MANY TREES that bloom in the spring and turn beautiful colors in the fall. The view those times of the year is incredible, and I always look forward to it. Several years ago, we had a bad snow and ice event that became treacherous in certain parts of town. It appeared suddenly and by the time I got to our neighborhood, I couldn't even make it up the first little incline. I had to park somewhere on level ground and a good neighbor who had a Jeep was transporting folks to their homes where we remained for two days. The road was so icy we couldn't make it down the winding, curvy hill out of the neighborhood. Guess what? I did not enjoy my view that day, because there were no flowers blooming and no brilliant leaves anywhere to be seen. I don't mind staying in the house if it's of my choosing, but I'm not a very contented individual when it's forced upon me.

I was reminded of that time recently as I was reading this passage of Scripture. The Bible talks about the road to eternal life being a narrow road. In the past, throughout my life, I never thought much about that scripture other than it was a road and I had to stay on it. Have you ever driven I-70 across Kansas? You can see a perfectly straight line of interstate highway miles and miles ahead of you. The only obstacle might be an occasional tumble weed. As I considered the struggles and the trials we go through in our Christian walk and the circumstances that sometimes

surround the life of a child of God, I realize this road is not always a straight road. Through the eyes of the Spirit, I could see along that road there are thorn bushes, sometimes there are trees that have fallen across the road, and branches that are hanging down and have cluttered the pathway. Sometimes, things have fallen on the road that we have to kick out of the way or we must grab a spiritual chainsaw to cut the big trees into logs so that we can clear the path before us. The Bible doesn't say it's an easy path or a clear path, it just says it's a narrow path.

So just as we must be patient for beauty to appear in our natural landscape, we must have the same determination to wait it out on this straight and narrow spiritual path that we walk. Once the obstructions have been cleared, we can once again see our way to forge ahead toward our final destination.

God, I thank you, that even when there are obstacles on this road we travel, You lead and guide us safely through. We are able to be overcomers because of Your power that lives in us.

~Paula

My Bible Reading Plan

☐ Day 232   Jeremiah 40–42
☐ Day 233   Jeremiah 43–45
☐ Day 234   Jeremiah 46–48
☐ Day 235   Jeremiah 49–52
☐ Day 236   Lamentations 1–3
☐ Day 237   Lamentations 4–5
☐ Day 238   Ezekiel 1–3

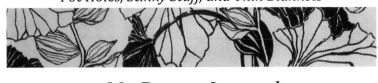

My Prayer Journal

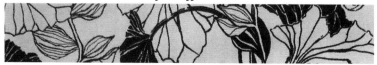

Better Together

*Moses said to the Lord, "Pardon your servant, Lord. I have never
been eloquent, neither in the past nor since you have spoken to
your servant. I am slow of speech and tongue* (Exodus 4:10 NIV).

MY HUSBAND AND I WERE WATCHING an old episode
of the Andy Griffith show. Many who are reading this devotion will remember the one to which I'm referring. It
was where Barney had the solo tenor part with the choir.
As he approached the microphone during one particular
choir practice, he stood strong and tall, beaming with
confidence at his ability. Everyone quickly realized, of
course, that the confidence which was oozing from every fiber of his being, originating from the pride that he
could sing this solo part, rested solely in his own mind,
but not in anyone else's. The choir director determined
at this point that whatever steps had to be taken to prevent it, this could not happen, because Barney was not a
good singer. A replacement was found, but Barney's feelings were wounded. In the end, it all worked out, as a trio
formed, and with two other singers it sounded amazing.
This proves that at certain times there is safety in numbers and companionship, and during those times being
solo is not a great idea. It reminds me of something I read
one time that was an awesome reality. Snowflakes are
fragile, but when they stick together they can stop traffic.
Isn't that great?

Always remember God is strong in us when we are
weak, but He also uses others to strengthen us in our
weaknesses. This happened when God called Moses to
deliver the children of Israel and he resisted, because he

could not speak well enough. He was fearful he couldn't do what God was asking. God was patient with Moses and told him: "Okay, Moses, I'll provide a mouthpiece for you in the form of Aaron, your brother." That's precisely what God did. It wasn't the only time God made provision for Moses by sending people alongside to be helpers in ministry. Every time Moses wasn't good enough to sing the solo, so to speak, and each time his arms became weak, others came alongside Moses to speak and to hold up his arms. God always knew when two was better than one. He knows it as well in our lives—He always makes a way.

God, remind me that when I can't handle the task alone,
You provide all I ever need to be complete.

~Paula

My Bible Reading Plan

☐ Day 239   Ezekiel 4–6
☐ Day 240   Ezekiel 7–9
☐ Day 241   Ezekiel 10–12
☐ Day 242   Ezekiel 13–15
☐ Day 243   Ezekiel 16–18
☐ Day 244   Ezekiel 19–21
☐ Day 245   Ezekiel 22–24

My Prayer Journal

_____

_____

_____

_____

_____

_____

_____

_____

_____

_____

_____

_____

_____

_____

_____

_____

_____

_____

_____

_____

_____

_____

_____

_____

Silence Is Golden

A time to tear, and a time to sew; A time to keep silence, and a time to speak (Ecclesiastes 3:7 NKJV).

I SAW A FUNNY MEME ON ONE OF THE SOCIAL MEDIA SITES recently: "Silence is golden. Duct tape is silver." Do you ever find yourself talking and then suddenly just stop and realize what you're saying? Or does the Holy Spirit ever convict you of the words coming forth from your mouth? It happens to me quite often and I realize maybe that duct tape would come in handy to keep me from verbalizing some of those negative thoughts. Either way— golden silence or silver duct tape—I need to keep those knee-jerk reactions and negative thoughts from coming out of my mouth.

For example, the other day I was talking about a certain situation and I said to someone, "I know what's going to happen. I guarantee you they are not going to admit they are wrong and I know they will not change their mind." The situation did not turn out like I predicted it would, and that's usually the case with my predictions. Do you know what my problem was? I began to realize I was speaking my conclusion based on my circumstance.

Do you find yourself doing the same thing? It's easy to fall into that trap. The problem is we think with our carnal minds and we judge things on the only natural solution that can result from a circumstance or situation. I'm sure glad our heavenly Father doesn't make a conclusion based on my circumstance. If He did, I promise you I would be in

a lot of trouble most of the time. So, when I have prayed about my situation, the right solution is something I'm going to leave to the God I pray to and know that He knows the way it will turn out. It's sure a lot less stressful that way.

God, You are the one who handles the outcome and I trust You completely. I thank You that You see and know how to do all that needs to be done.

~Paula

My Bible Reading Plan

☐ Day 246   Ezekiel 25–27
☐ Day 247   Ezekiel 28–30
☐ Day 248   Ezekiel 31–33
☐ Day 249   Ezekiel 34–36
☐ Day 250   Ezekiel 37–39
☐ Day 251   Ezekiel 40–42
☐ Day 252   Ezekiel 43–45

My Prayer Journal

Sunglasses

I pray that the eyes of your heart may be enlightened in order that you may know the hope to which He has called you, the riches of His glorious inheritance in His holy people (Ephesians 1:18 NIV).

IN MY CAR, I KEEP A PAIR OF SUNGLASSES I am protective over. I spent a lot of money over time buying the most inexpensive ones I could find and having to replace them way too often because they would scratch or smudge. Finally, my optometrist convinced me of the importance of "real" sunglasses. Our eyes are sensitive. Remembering to wear a pair of high quality sunglasses can help to keep you safe from the sun's damaging rays. Here's what else I learned. Prolonged exposure to sun can lead to a variety of ailments. Some are simply painful or irritating, but others can be deadly serious. Better sunglasses protect against "blue light" from the solar spectrum, which could increase your risk of macular degeneration. They protect your eyelids from developing skin cancer. Bright sunlight can be a trigger for migraines and severe headaches. Wearing good sunglasses can help reduce both the frequency and intensity of these painful occurrences. Even if you're not prone to these things, wearing sunglasses when out in the sun can help reduce eyestrain and fatigue.

I began to think about this in the life of a Christian. Many times, the things we see are so irritating, or so uncomfortable spiritually, that it is easy to be distressed. Just as we do in the natural, why can't we put on spiritual sunglasses? It would allow God to cover the eyes of our

hearts, shield our spirits, and our minds. That way, when we see something that causes us to squint our eyes because it's hard to observe, the covering of the Lord would act as spiritual sunglasses to keep the glare from being too distracting. It would help us see a little bit clearer whenever things seem so glaringly obvious to the point they hurt our spiritual eyes.

Tragically, the eyes of many Christians don't see very well. Often, our spiritual vision is blinded by the glare of what our physical eyes see. Our spiritual eyes must not be cloudy and blinded. We must not let the sun of envy or bitterness rise in the sky of our hearts, or its harsh brightness will blind us from the fact of God's goodness. We must be reminded to look again, and this time with the eyes of faith. When we finally see clearly, we can shout, "God is good!"

God, help me see clearly through the eyes of the Spirit, so that I will not be distracted or discouraged by what I observe in the flesh. Help me to keep my eyes clearly focused upon You and Your goodness.

~Paula

My Bible Reading Plan

My Prayer Journal

Thank You for the Veggies

I know what it is to be in need, and I know what it is to have plenty. I have learned the secret of being content in any and every situation, whether well fed or hungry, whether living in plenty or in want (Philippians 4:12 NIV).

I HATE VEGETABLES. I've tried most of my life to like them, but I prefer not to eat them. I have the greatest mom and she tried her best when I was young to get me to eat vegetables, but I just wasn't having it. As any good mom does, she fed me what I would eat, so I wouldn't starve. As a kid, I had no filter or wisdom, obviously. I didn't realize then that if I would just try what was on my plate, I would probably find some part of the meal that was enjoyable, or at least enough to keep me satisfied. What would I do? I would sit, I wouldn't eat, and then I would become hungrier and angrier. When I reached a certain age, I think my parents realized after raising two other daughters that they had to choose their battles, and me not eating my veggies wasn't one they wanted to fight.

My husband, who loves anything you put in front of him, gets to deal with my eating habits. As ministers, we travel a lot as a family. I learned quickly after our move to Michigan that no one really wanted my opinion about where I wanted to eat. Let's face it, no one else wants to eat chicken or pizza for every meal. I'll never forget one of our first ministry opportunities in Michigan. The pastor had us meet him at a Mediterranean restaurant. You might as well have told me we were on our way to eat pickled pigs' feet. My attitude didn't improve when all I saw was a foreign language and

the word "kabob" on every other line of the menu. What did I do? I ordered the closest thing to plain old grilled chicken I could find.

That day I didn't get the food I wanted right away. Over time I learned if I could wait, I would receive something I did desire. I also had to learn to be thankful for the blessings I received in the waiting. Isn't this how we are so often with God? We see an answer after we've prayed, and the answer is the farthest thing from what we wanted. Often, if we wait just a little longer, God always provides something that is much more satisfying. We must learn to be thankful for the things God provides, even when it doesn't look like something we desire. He will never let us go hungry or leave us alone. We must be content no matter our situation and trust that He is for us and not against us.

Lord, thank you for blessings that do not always look like what I desire. Help me to be content with what I receive. I trust that You have my best interest at heart, no matter what my answer looks like. I will not worry but always trust that I am in Your hands.

~Tara

My Bible Reading Plan

☐ Day 260   Hosea 7–9
☐ Day 261   Hosea 10–12
☐ Day 262   Hosea 13–14
☐ Day 263   Joel 1–3
☐ Day 264   Amos 1–3
☐ Day 265   Amos 4–6
☐ Day 266   Amos 7–9

My Prayer Journal

The Good Doctor

And those who know Your name will put their trust in You,
for You, Lord, have not forsaken those who seek you
(Psalms 9:10 NKJV).

MY 3-YEAR-OLD SMASHED HIS THUMB IN A CABINET DOOR! It was one of those spring-loaded doors, so it got him really good. His nail started turning black instantly. Having raised two other children, I've seen just about everything, so I'm not one to rush to the doctor for every little thing. I responded with lots of boo-boo kisses and cuddles and a "let's give it the weekend and see how it looks." By Sunday, it was swollen and completely bruised. Add to that, I heard horror stories of other cases like these at church that made me super paranoid. So, bright and early Monday morning off to the doctor we went. By this point, he wouldn't even let me touch that arm, because it hurt his hand to move it. The doctor came in and totally reassured me nothing was broken, and this was pretty common. HOWEVER, he would feel better and my son would feel better if we let him drain the nail and relieve some pressure. I went into full blown panic mode. All I could think was how in the world was I going to get Lucas to be still so they could drain his thumb? I was prepared to hold him down with all my might and do everything possible to keep him still long enough for the doctor to do this super simple procedure. I had a movie playing on my iPad, games ready on my phone, and was holding a book for him to look at, all in efforts to keep him distracted. I knew there would be screaming and gnashing of teeth, because they were about to jab a needle into his thumb. I saw the

needle; he took Lucas' hand and I squeezed my eyes shut, prepared for the worst. Within a few seconds, I peeked to see what was wrong, because I didn't think he had started yet. I was shocked to see he had in fact started. There was no screaming, crying, or even trying to wiggle free. Lucas was just watching. Every now and then, I would see a look of concern flash across his eyes, but he would look at the doctor, then go back to observing. Lucas has been with this same doctor from the week he came home from the hospital. He knows him and trusts him. He knew that he would not be hurt by this man. He was totally at peace, because he was in the hands of a good doctor.

How much better off would we be if we placed all our trust in our very own heavenly physician? The one who formed us and knows us inside and out. If we could ever be like my little man and keep our eyes on our good doctor, knowing he will never cause any harm to us and will never forsake us, how much more peace would that bring. How much better life is when we learn to trust in the GOOD DOCTOR!

~Melinda

My Bible Reading Plan

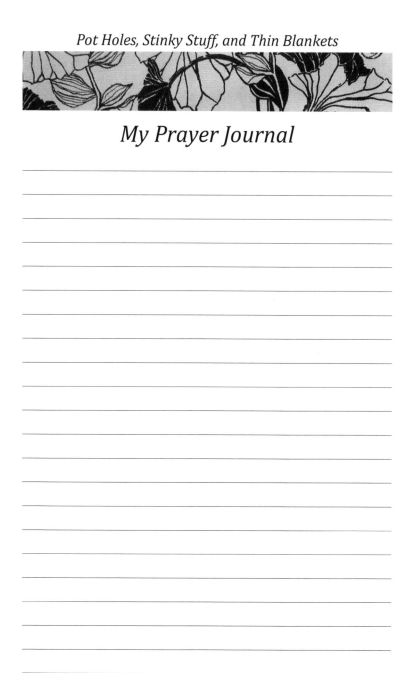

My Prayer Journal

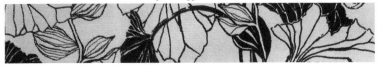

The Yard of the Month—Not!

Let your light so shine before men, that they may see your good works and glorify your Father in heaven
(Matthew 5:16 NKJV).

I'VE HEARD IT SAID THE BEST WAY TO DIG A GARDEN, or work in the garden, is to put on wide-brimmed straw hat and some old clothes. Then, with a hoe in one hand and a glass of lemonade in the other tell someone else where to dig! This piece of advice reminded me of something I saw in my own neighborhood.

A house in our neighborhood was built several years ago. It's a nice brick home on the outside, but the yard never quite looked like it should. I'm not talking about an immaculate, spotless yard-of-the-year award home; I'm talking just simple green grass. The yard is steep, and every time grass seed was sown, rain would wash most of it right into the gutter. Because of the way the yard looked, I was never fond of that house. Someone recently bought the house and landscaped the yard with sod. Wow! The addition of the beautiful landscaping now makes the entire house more appealing.

Let's compare that scenario to the life of a believer. We often convince ourselves it's not important by what or whom we're surrounded. I don't think it's unimportant that you and I are perceived to be connected to what we take part in or with whom we participate in those things. I know I'm at risk of being misunderstood here, because I understand you shouldn't try to please everybody, and I know it's wrong to pass judgment when you don't have

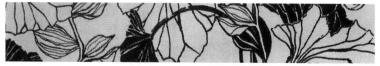

all the facts. Believe me, you do need to live a life that is pleasing to God. We miss the opportunity many times to reach an individual, because they look at things and judge us to be less than the kind of Christian by whom they want to be influenced. It may not be fair or right, but unfortunately, it's truth. We know when our hearts are pure and right before God, but others may look and find unattractive the "first impression" we make; that totally closes the door for being a witness. So, just as the rather unappealing surroundings of the house in my neighborhood kept me from having any desire to care what was on the inside of that house, I don't want my life to cause anyone to turn away from Christ because of my surroundings. Do you?

Father, help me to please you with my life, not so I'll look good to others, but that I may be a faithful and true servant who attracts those in need of Your presence.

~Paula

My Bible Reading Plan

My Prayer Journal

_____

_____

_____

_____

_____

_____

_____

_____

_____

_____

_____

_____

_____

_____

_____

_____

_____

_____

_____

_____

_____

_____

_____

_____

The Way

Whether you turn to the right or to the left, your ears will hear a voice behind you, saying, This is the way; walk in it (Isaiah 30:21 NIV).

I'M ONE OF THOSE PEOPLE WHO IS DIRECTIONALLY CHALLENGED. If I'm going somewhere and you tell me go north or go south, most of the time, I don't have a clue how to figure that out unless I have a directional device in front of me. The way I find my direction is to ask for landmarks along the way. I need to know to turn left at the gas station on the corner or go to the third red light and take a right. No, even that doesn't work. It has to be turn right at the red light that has a big McDonald's on the corner. I've always been amazed at those folks who can stand anywhere, spin them around, make them close their eyes, and when they open their eyes they can point north. I know I'm just displaying my lack of knowledge here, but I'm sorry, I don't get how they do that. Wait a minute and let me redeem myself a little bit. If I see the sun rising, I can point east or if I see the sun setting, I can point west. But without the rising and setting of the sun, the best I can do for accurate direction is "up and down."

When I think about my life from the spiritual aspect, I realize I don't have any sense of direction spiritually either if I'm trying to make it on my own. I have no choice but to follow Jesus. If I don't follow Him, I lose my direction, I lose my guidance. I lose my spiritual navigation system. I don't know which decision to make, which landmarks will lead me down the right path. But I love that He promises never to leave us nor forsake us. We don't have

135

to worry about losing our direction as long as we follow the landmarks and guidelines He has set forth for us in His Word. I believe we have to always remember who we are following and remember He knows the path and the direction we need to go. I don't know about you, but I'd rather the GPS I rely on be my God-Positioning-System than my Global-Positioning System any day of the week.

God, I trust my path to You. Lead and guide me with
Your hand of mercy and direction. I depend on You
for each step I take.

~Paula

My Bible Reading Plan

☐ Day 281   Matthew 1–3
☐ Day 282   Matthew 4–6
☐ Day 283   Matthew 7–9
☐ Day 284   Matthew 10–12
☐ Day 285   Matthew 13–15
☐ Day 286   Matthew 16–18
☐ Day 287   Matthew 19–21

My Prayer Journal

What Is Spring?

For still the vision awaits its appointed time; it hastens to the end—it will not lie. If it seems slow, wait for it; it will surely come; it will not delay (Habakkuk 2:3 ESV).

I LIVE IN MICHIGAN. If you've never been to Michigan, you may not be familiar with the extreme highs and mainly lows of our weather. The first year we moved to Michigan, spring was beautiful! We were fishing in the pond behind our house, going for walks, enjoying the sun, and we had put away our coats by the beginning of April. This year has not been so fortunate. We had three inches of snow on the first day of spring! The next day it was in the 60s again. Now as I look out the window in mid-April, there is frost and white snow as far as the eye can see.

I've learned quickly this year that the name of the season doesn't always go along with the weather pattern. That sounds silly, but living in Michigan will change what you've always believed about the weather. Being raised in Tennessee, we knew once spring hit, so did the sun, shorts, and sandals. The other day here in Michigan, I saw one girl with warm winter boots and her friend walked beside her wearing shorts and flip flops. I think they were just as confused as the rest of us feel.

I found an important lesson during these crazy weather patterns. Right now it is spring, but if you look out my window, your natural eyes would tell you it is obviously winter. Sometimes God moves us into a new season, but that new season doesn't always present itself with new

and amazing circumstances right away. Many times, this "new season" God is bringing us looks a great deal like the season we've been through the last six months of our lives. Often, I look out the window and lose hope that the grass will be green, and my son will be running outside playing again. Just as I lose hope, God reminds me He's promised something better—it just may take longer than I would like. Regardless the name of your season, God is doing a new thing in His time, even if that new thing looks a lot like the same thing you've had. We must remind ourselves God's promises for us are Yes and Amen! We must also take time to remember God works everything together for our good, even if that means our "winter" or old season is extended. There is always hope for a new season.

Lord, help me to know my new season is coming. Don't let me lose hope when what I see doesn't match what you've promised in Your Word. I know you are faithful and will not abandon me in the wilderness. Amen.

~Tara

My Bible Reading Plan

☐ Day 288   Matthew 22–24
☐ Day 289   Matthew 25–28
☐ Day 290   Mark 1–3
☐ Day 291   Mark 4–6
☐ Day 292   Mark 7–9
☐ Day 293   Mark 10–12
☐ Day 294   Mark 13–16

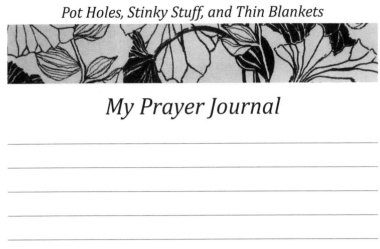

My Prayer Journal

Waves

Do you not fear Me? says the Lord.
Will you not tremble at My presence,
Who have placed the sand as the bound of the sea,
By a perpetual decree, that it cannot pass beyond it?
And though its waves toss to and fro,
Yet they cannot prevail;
Though they roar, yet they cannot pass over it
(Jeremiah 5:22 NKJV).

I WENT ON A GIRLS' VACATION TO THE BEACH with my closest friends. We spent most days sleeping on the beach with brief times of getting into the ocean to cool off. One day it was just unbearably hot, so we spent a lot of time in the water. The current wasn't too bad, but the waves were so, so, so strong! I was trying hard to dig my toes into the sand and hold my ground, but over and over I kept getting knocked down by those waves! I finally decided to lift my feet and just swim with the waves instead of letting them knock me over again and again. What seemed like a stone wall constantly hitting me in the face when I had my toes dug in, suddenly became this amazing force lifting me and carrying me on top of the waves instead of knocking me under them. All I had to do was lift my feet and let go!

It occurred to me our walk with the Lord can be similar to my experience with the waves. Sometimes life, or our future, seems so scary that we dig our toes into the sand to prepare or prevent getting "knocked over." If we could just lift our feet and let God carry us, He will keep

us on top of the waves that come crashing down. It will still be scary, and you may have to remind yourself to let go. When I saw those waves building far out there, it was still intimidating, and I wanted to dig my toes in, but I had to remind myself, "Let it carry you." Sure enough, when I fought the urge to dig in, I floated above. God won't always take the waves away, but He will for sure carry you through them.

It's good to know we don't have to be knocked over by life's waves when they come along. If we just trust the one in charge of those waves and let him carry us through, we will make it!

Father, thank you for teaching me you are there to catch me and carry me through the waves of fear and doubt that try to overtake me. Your hand is as close as my surrender to Your strength in my weakness.

~Melinda

My Bible Reading Plan

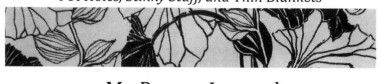

My Prayer Journal

The World Can't Give It

You will show me the path of life; In Your presence is fullness of joy; at Your right hand are pleasures forevermore
(Psalm 16:11 NKJV).

You may have noticed many of my devotions refer to songs and music, and there's a reason for that. Music has always been a powerful way for me to find encouragement and strength. It's as if the right song can fill my gas tank when it's running on empty. Most of the time, I sing to myself. Many times, my memories take me back to my younger days and songs I grew up with. Here's one for you—it's an old song that was fun to sing as a child—an up-tempo, hand-clapping song. The words are not hard to learn, and it carries great truth:

> *This joy that I have, the world didn't give it to me.*
> *This joy that I have, the world didn't give it to me.*
> *This joy that I have, the world didn't give it to me.*
> *The world didn't give it and the world can't take it away!*
> *This peace that I have, the world didn't give it to me.*
> *This peace that I have, the world didn't give it to me.*
> *This peace that I have, the world didn't give it to me.*
> *The world didn't give it and the world can't take it away!*

The song is one of those you can add as many verses you want by changing one word from joy to peace or to love or whatever you need. Just fill in the blank!

It may be a simple song with simple words, and it may seem irrelevant to some, but it's so true that we live in a world where things have gone absolutely crazy and there appears to be no boundaries. Trouble is on every side and it seems hopeless to "hope" anymore. People are searching for peace, love, joy, and security in the middle of this society where tragedy seems to be the norm. Those things can't be found in the natural. There's not enough money to purchase these things and no one wields enough power to demand them. They are as elusive as the wind, or like trying to catch a single raindrop as it's falling from the sky to the parched ground. But, there is a Savior who overcame the world, and who still helps us overcome the struggles in our own personal world no matter what they are. Praise God for the good news!

Heavenly Father, I thank You that security can still be found in You. You are joy, peace, hope, and any verse we need you to be.

~Paula

My Bible Reading Plan

My Prayer Journal

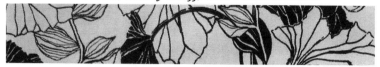

Think on These Things

Finally, brothers and sisters, whatever is true, whatever is noble, whatever is right, whatever is pure, whatever is lovely, whatever is admirable—if anything is excellent or praiseworthy—think about such things
(Philippians 4:8 NIV).

I WAS CONFRONTED WITH A SITUATION THAT WAS FRUSTRATING. It came from a source totally unexpected and it caught me completely off guard. It happened first thing in the morning and, let me preface this by saying it wasn't my husband. It affected me in an unhealthy way. I try hard to always keep things in perspective, but honestly, perspective was difficult to come by that morning. I left the house to run some errands and keep several appointments, all the while trying to talk myself out of this frustration. As I was driving from one place to the other, I found myself in such a state that everything was frustrating me! The traffic, the red lights, the other drivers, the sun glaring off the windshield—you name it—I was frustrated by it. I had to stop at the gas station, because my car was below empty, and as I stood there, I hardly had the patience to wait for the gas nozzle to click off. Enough was enough! As I got back into the car, I put my head down on the steering wheel and with tears in my eyes, I asked the Lord to please help me get over that which was affecting every step I took and every thought going through my mind. Thankfully, He heard my plea.

When I returned home later, out of curiosity I decided to research what happens to your body when you are

overcome by anxiety and frustration. Are you ready for this? Heart palpitations, neck tension, headaches, chest pain, upset stomach, and these are just a few. The list was long. What do we do to overcome these feelings? We have to stop listening to ourselves and start talking to ourselves. We have to preach to ourselves, lecture ourselves, exhort ourselves. We cannot overcome anxiety unless we learn to replace worried thoughts with worthy thoughts, thoughts that come directly from the mind of the God of peace. We must do as Paul said and take up the practice of thinking. We must ask God to redirect our thinking toward His Word and His thoughts. It may take a while, but it will eventually calm those pounding hearts and tense muscles when we speak the truth of His Word into our hearts and minds.

Lord, I know frustrating things are a part of life, but help me remember I can overcome these things through the power of Your Word.

~Paula

My Bible Reading Plan

My Prayer Journal

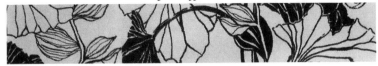

Was He Watching?

When I said, My foot is slipping, your unfailing love, Lord, supported me. When anxiety was great within me, your consolation brought me joy (Psalms 94:18-19 NIV).

DO YOU HAVE THOSE DAYS? One of those dreaded days when you honestly feel totally, completely inadequate and incapable of handling even the smallest of situations? Please don't be disappointed in me, but I have, and I do. Thankfully, not every day, but more often than I'd like to admit. Let's see, when was the last one I had? Oh yeah, yesterday! Nothing bad happened, nobody made me feel bad, it was all me. Here's how it played out. Long day, tired, listening, thinking, talking, praying, caring, loving, mothering, wife-ing (I'm not sure that's a real word but it should be), grand-mothering, etc., etc. Let me say these are all wonderful blessings I'm so thankful I have been allowed the privilege to be a part. I pulled into the driveway, shut off the engine, put my head on the steering wheel, and cried. Yes, I had the passing thought the neighbors might be looking out the windows, but I overcame that concern and kept crying. The conversation went something like this: "God, I don't think I'm the right person. Did you turn Your head to look at someone else who was the one and I accidentally slipped by into the wrong place? Am I really supposed to be the one doing all this? Please tell me it wasn't a mistake."

Sorry if I'm being too real, but as a woman, it would be a rare story if it's never happened to you. If not, I would love to talk to you and find out your secret. Let me say

to the rest of you, if you are kept in the Master's hand and your whole being is sold out to Him, I assure you God didn't look away or close His eyes, and allow you to get in the wrong line. He has a plan for you, He has always had a plan, and He knows how to wrap His soothing arms around each troubled heart. Just as He reminded me of this passage in the Bible, He will remind you, too, that His joy is the consolation prize when you stand in the middle of anxiousness. His great love will be the support you need when you feel like your feet are slipping out from underneath you. Be encouraged, get a good night's sleep, and when you open your eyes tomorrow, declare this is the day the Lord has made. We can, and we will rejoice in Him for His provisions.

Dear God, thank you for choosing me. Regardless of those days when I wonder why or how, I know You trust me with it, and You enable me to do what I have been chosen to do with peace of mind and abundant joy.
What a privilege!

~Paula

My Bible Reading Plan

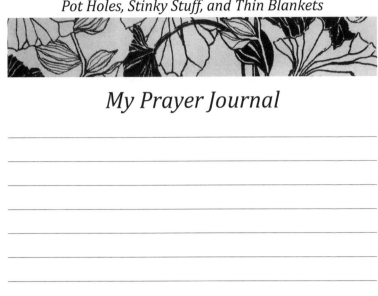

My Prayer Journal

_____

_____

_____

_____

_____

_____

_____

_____

_____

_____

_____

_____

_____

_____

_____

_____

_____

_____

_____

_____

_____

_____

_____

_____

_____

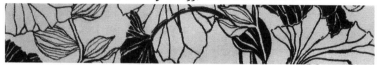

Weakness Made Strong

He gives power to the weak, and to those that have no might He increases strength (Isaiah 40:29 NKJV).

FOR A WHILE EVERYONE WAS TELLING CHUCK NOR-RIS JOKES and they still pop up on social media sites. I saw one a few days ago that was so dumb I had to laugh. The joke was that Superman wears Chuck Norris pajamas. Ok, that was really bad, but these jokes are geared toward the strength of one man and how he overcomes every obstacle and demands attention, awe, and respect.

"I discovered an astonishing truth: God is attracted to weakness. He can't resist those who humbly and honestly admit how desperately they need Him. Our weakness, in fact, makes room for His power." —Jim Cymbala

I recently saw this quote by Jim Cymbala, and it spoke into my spirit. It was one of those days when the weaknesses in my life seemed to be magnified beyond the actual reality of truth. I was thinking about all the frailties and insecurities we have as human beings, and especially of how we are constantly reminded of what the world's views are on these issues. All you have to do is turn on the television to watch the news, the talk shows, and the various documentaries to quickly pick up on the message of society—that only the strongest, fastest, most talented individuals who are ahead of the game of life survive. Other individuals, regretfully, are woefully left behind, forgotten, and are the losers. The weak don't survive and have a hard time finding their place in society.

What about weakness related to our spiritual lives? I was reminded of so many scriptures on that subject, but of all that came to my remembrance, it seems the Bible does not say He gives strength to the strong, or more power to the powerful, as the world tells us. It does tell us He completes who we are and what we are. He knows what the missing part is, and He knows what the component is that's lacking in our lives. His Word reminds us it's not by our own power or our own strength that anything is done through or in us, but it is all accomplished by His Spirit. I'm so glad God provides equal opportunity to all, no matter how weak or strong we may be. He completes everything in us that is lacking. Praise God!

Father, I thank You my weakness is not a detriment to what I am in You. Help me remember I am made strong as I put my faith and trust in You.

~Paula

My Bible Reading Plan

☐ Day 323   Romans 13–16
☐ Day 324   1 Corinthians 1–3
☐ Day 325   1 Corinthians 4–6
☐ Day 326   1 Corinthians 7–9
☐ Day 327   1 Corinthians 10–12
☐ Day 328   1 Corinthians 13–16
☐ Day 329   2 Corinthians 1–3

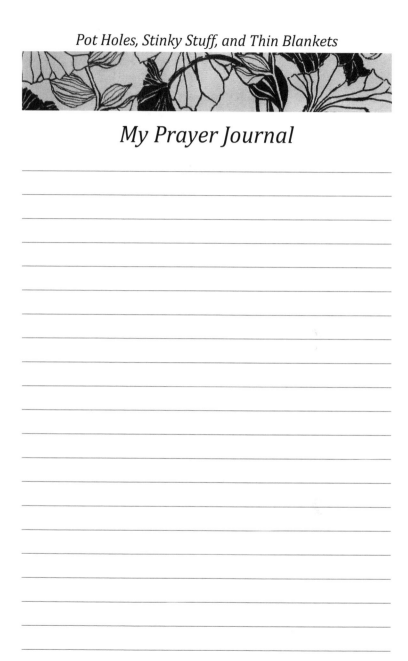

My Prayer Journal

The Order of Things

Commit to the Lord whatever you do, and he will establish your plans (Proverbs 16:3 NIV).

ONE NIGHT ABOUT 11:30 I FINALLY HAD ALL MY LAUNDRY FINISHED and folded with hanging up clothes ready to distribute to various closets, towels to various bathrooms, sheets and other items ready to be put in their places, everything neatly stacked.

As I just stood there looking at it all, I was trying to decide what to put up first. I mean after all, at that time of night it's all about the least amount of steps and the most expeditious way to hurry and get it done so I can get to bed. Then as I just stood there staring at it all the thought very forcefully came to my mind "JUST GRAB SOMETHING AND PUT IT UP. IT ALL HAS TO BE PUT UP ANYWAY SO WHAT DOES IT MATTER WHAT YOU GRAB FIRST?"

Well, as it tends to happen with me, the Spirit of God touched my heart and I felt Him impress upon me the truth that many times we view God's "system" or His workings in the same way.

We have a whole countertop or basket full of life's issues and burdens that need to be put in place, so to speak, or put in order. But then we don't always trust Him with what He does first and what He does last. We don't always trust his order of things. We are picky about what seems to be the thing at the top of our priority list with God. Perhaps it may be "God, why did you give me that

raise on my job first instead of saving my husband? The raise could wait. It's not that desperate. But my husband really needs salvation." But we must let God look at all our circumstances and make the decision about when and where and the order.

God, all these things that are needed in my life I know You will take care of in Your perfect timing and Your perfect way. Help me remember that.

~Paula

My Bible Reading Plan

☐   Day 330   2 Corinthians 4–6
☐   Day 331   2 Corinthians 7–9
☐   Day 332   2 Corinthians 10–13
☐   Day 333   Galatians 1–3
☐   Day 334   Galatians 4–6
☐   Day 335   Ephesians 1–3
☐   Day 336   Ephesians 4–6

Pot Holes, Stinky Stuff, and Thin Blankets

My Prayer Journal

The Dressmaker

Then Peter arose and went with them. When he had come,
they brought him to the upper room. And all the widows
stood by him weeping, showing the tunics and garments
which Dorcas had made while she was with them
(Acts 9:39 NKJV).

FEW THINGS THAT I BUY ARE EVER A PERFECT FIT. I
have always had a small waist line which, unfortunately,
is out of proportion with the rest of my body. Because of
that, most things I buy have to be altered. Thankfully, I
can usually take care of the alterations myself. You may
find this rather humorous, but when I turned 16 years
of age, which has been more than a few years ago, most
young people my age were asking for their first car. My
plea was for a nice sewing machine in a big beautiful cabinet. I'm talking about the Cadillac of all sewing machines,
not just some cheap sewing machine you could go to any
store and purchase. The one I wanted could be bought
in stores where they sold only sewing machines. This
desire no doubt came from watching my mother sew. I
was totally fascinated as she turned lifeless, unformed,
odd-shaped pieces of cloth into a dress. I remember the
excitement of getting to high school and enrolling for
my first semester of home economics. I wanted to learn
to sew. My first garment was a skirt and, it was pitiful!
I have no idea how someone could mess something up
that badly, but with the help of a patient home economics
teacher and some experience, I finally mastered the art
of sewing. As a teenager, when I wanted a new dress to

wear to church on Sunday morning, I would stay up Saturday night sewing to make that happen.

My passion is valuing women for the gifts God has placed on each of them. You will possibly see it woven into many of my stories when you are reading my books. The Bible lets us know Dorcas had a gift for sewing, and when she died, her friends wanted Peter to know how valuable her life had been and how she was loved. I'm sure she had many other talents, but this is the one mentioned in the Bible. This tells me her gift was important and valued. Remember to do all to the glory of God, whatever you do. He uses it to touch others' lives in more ways than you can imagine.

God, thank you because I have gifts given to me that are hand designed by You. They are special, and I cherish them and stand in awe of them.

~Paula

My Bible Reading Plan

☐ Day 337   Philippians 1–4
☐ Day 338   Colossians 1–4
☐ Day 339   1 Thessalonians 1–3
☐ Day 340   1 Thessalonians 4–5
☐ Day 341   2 Thessalonians 1–3
☐ Day 342   1 Timothy 1–3
☐ Day 343   1 Timothy 4–6

My Prayer Journal

The Wrong Person

And Moses said unto the Lord, O my Lord, I am not elo-
quent, neither heretofore, nor since thou hast spoken unto
thy servant: but I am slow of speech, and of a
slow tongue (Exodus 4:10 KJV).

I WAS WITH SOMEONE WHO WAS CONSIDERING A CA-
REER CHANGE, but still in the beginning phase of deciding if it would lead to a more long-term security for the
future. Many of the reasons you can imagine, such as sal-
ary, fulfillment, qualifications, etc. The person then made
this statement: "I can do the job. I'm very qualified. It's
exciting to think about the possibility; I know I could be
fulfilled and successful if I do it." I thought to myself how
amazing it would be to feel that way.

I began to think first about myself and how I have often
felt about opportunities that have come my way, many of
them not of my own choosing. I was reminded of Moses
and his story. Confidence was certainly not a word you
would use to describe the way he felt. As many of us do,
we have excuses like Moses had before God on why he
could not fulfill his calling. First, Moses' response to his
calling was to say, "Who am I?" Second, Moses pleaded a
lack of knowledge. Moses' third excuse to God was he did
not believe he had the power to fulfill the calling God had
requested of him. Moses' fourth excuse to God was that
speaking and leadership abilities were lacking. I'm afraid
I'm more like Moses than I'd like to admit.

After it's all said and done, God didn't call me to be
qualified, He called me to be willing. He didn't call me

because I was the best, or the one at the front of the line jumping up and down waving my arms and saying pick me, pick me. He called me, because I was the one at the back of the line, though willing, who wouldn't feel qualified to step forward and volunteer.

I'm reminded of something I heard author and speaker Jill Briscoe say years ago and it was that we pray many times, "God give me the courage to obey you," and God says, "Obey Me and I'll give you the courage." Pretty well sums it all up, don't you think?

God, I thank You that You take unqualified and unlikely candidates who are willing, or even hesitant sometimes, and You use them anyway to bring glory to You.

~Paula

My Bible Reading Plan

My Prayer Journal

Perspective

Let us lay us aside every weight, and the sin which so easily ensnares us, and let us run with patience the race that is set before us (Hebrews 12:1 NKJV).

I HAVE ONE BROTHER AND ONE SISTER, both of whom I love very much. My sister began a weight loss journey a few years ago through surgery and a very strict eating lifestyle. She wouldn't mind me telling you that either. Health issues, amongst other things she would share with you, were a determining factor which forced her to make a drastic decision. I'm proud to tell you at present she has lost about 150 pounds and what an inspiration of perseverance she is to me. Well, with a somewhat embarrassed face, I have to tell you when I need to lose just a few pounds I moan and groan and complain because it's so hard to do. But, I used to try and encourage her with a simple statement my husband made to me many years ago after I'm pretty sure he grew tired of my whining about it, though he wouldn't tell you that. Or maybe more to the point, it was an action he suggested I take. He proceeded to tell me to survey the situation and add to each week instead of subtracting my loss and see where I would be in a few months if that was the direction I was heading. So I did and WOW! I had never thought about it like that. I decided perhaps I was being successful after all. It completely changed the way I viewed it.

I still think about that as I daily make my spiritual journey and how it is so applicable in that realm, as well. See I know I have shed the old carnality and taken on the

new creation in Christ, but too often I want to complain and whine about how hard it is to be "spiritual" and the difficulty of not acting and reacting in my fleshly mind-set. But, I must remind myself that difficult as it may be, I must not add things to my spiritual life that are going to be detrimental to my walk with my heavenly Father. To put back on fear and anxiety, or stubbornness and unforgiveness would be extra spiritual weight that I just don't want to start carrying around in my life again. Once He has subtracted that long list of whatever it may be you've been freed from, it's not good to add it back. It's sort of like with real weight—it may be harder to get rid of the second time around, or the third or fourth. I don't even want to go there. Do you?

Lord, help me to remember You are here and I can be healthy and whole with You as my encourager and my balance in this spiritual journey.

~Paula

My Bible Reading Plan

☐ Day 351   James 1–3
☐ Day 352   James 4–5
☐ Day 353   1 Peter 1–3
☐ Day 354   1 Peter 4–5
☐ Day 355   2 Peter 1–3
☐ Day 356   1 John 1–3
☐ Day 357   1 John 4–5

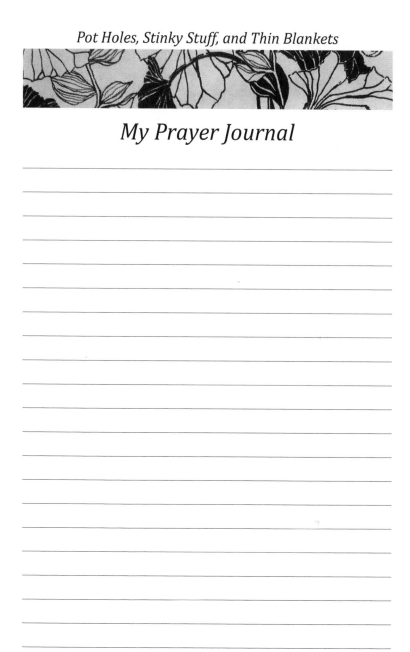

My Prayer Journal

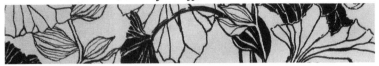

Opinion or Sin?

But You, O Lord, are a God full of compassion, and gracious, longsuffering and abundant in mercy and truth
(Psalms 86:15 NKJV).

I WAS TALKING TO SOMEONE ABOUT A SUBJECT recently which they felt very strongly about. And while I certainly could understand and even agree with much of their view on the subject, I was really taken aback by their attitude towards those who were not in complete agreement on the matter. Then a little while later in the conversation, I expressed sympathy for a person who had made a bad decision in their past and were trying to get their life back in right relationship with the Lord. Again, this person said to me, with a rather self-righteous attitude, I'm ashamed to say, "Well, they deserve it. They should have thought about that when they did it." I immediately began to think to myself about how this kind of attitude could possibly be pleasing to the Lord. I don't believe it could be. There was absolutely no attitude within this person that would point anyone towards a loving relationship with the God they serve. I walked away feeling very sad and honestly thinking I would never go to that person for help spiritually or otherwise.

It's certainly not wrong to take a stand for what is right if it lines up with the Word of God. But, we must beware of the danger of crossing over from strong opinion to sin, because I believe that is possible. The Bible speaks too much about love and forgiveness and compassion to believe it's not sin

when we take the rights away from a wise and all-knowing Father and take the judgment for these things into our own way of dealing with and looking at issues whatever they may be. Definitely fight for what is right, but do so with a heart that is in right relationship and attitude before the Lord. Otherwise, others may run away from you instead of running toward you and then you may find yourself fighting all alone. And that's no fun! It's much better to have allies than enemies.

Lord, let me always remember You are willing to help me when I stay in the right relationship with You. I want to draw people to You, not turn them away.

~Paula

My Bible Reading Plan

☐ Day 358   2 John, 3 John, Jude
☐ Day 359   Revelation 1–3
☐ Day 360   Revelation 4–6
☐ Day 361   Revelation 7–9
☐ Day 362   Revelation 10–12
☐ Day 363   Revelation 13–15
☐ Day 364   Revelation 16–18
☐ Day 365   Revelation 19–22

My Prayer Journal